THOUGHT-FORMS

Theosophy for the 21st Century

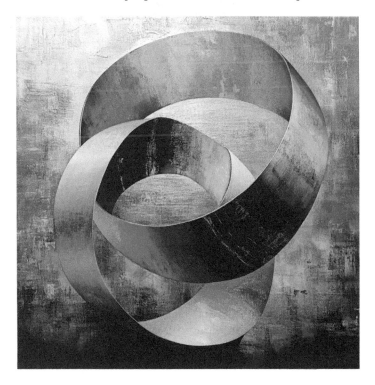

By Annie Besant and C.W. Leadbetter

THE THEOSOPHICAL PUBLISHING HOUSE LTD
38 GREAT ORMOND STREET, LONDON, W.C. 1
First Printed 1901
Reprint   1905
Reprint   1925

This special modern edition of Thought-Forms and Art-Forms contains original text by Annie Besant and C.W. Leadbetter as well as a ne introduction, updated prose, examples, and artworks for the modern 21ˢᵗ century reader.

Thought-Forms

1. High Spirituality.	1. Devotion mixed with Affection.	1. Devotion to a Noble Ideal.	1. Pure Religious Feeling.	1. Selfish Religious Feeling.
2. Religious Feeling, tinged with Fear.	2. Highest Intellect.	2. Strong Intellect.	2. Low type of Intellect.	2. Pride.
3. Sympathy.	3. Love for Humanity.	3. Unselfish Affection.	3. Selfish Affection.	3. Pure Affection.
4. Adaptability.	4. Jealousy.	4. Deceit.	4. Fear.	4. Depression
5. Selfishness.	5. Avarice.	5. Anger.	5. Sensuality.	5. Malice.

KEY TO THE MEANINGS OF COLOURS.
MEANING OF THE COLOURS

TABLE OF CONTENTS

Thought-Forms

THEOSOPHY FOR THE 21ST CENTURY

Theosophy is a spiritual movement that emerged in the late 19th century, blending elements of Eastern religions, Western esotericism, and mysticism into a comprehensive worldview. The movement sought to explore the hidden mysteries of life, the nature of the divine, and the spiritual evolution of humanity. In addition to Helena Petrovna Blavatsky, William Quan Judge, and Henry Steel Olcott, Annie Besant and Charles Webster Leadbeater were pivotal figures in the movement.

Theosophy, derived from the Greek words *theos* (god) and *sophia* (wisdom), signifies "divine wisdom." However, the roots of Theosophy can be traced back much earlier than the 19th century. Its conceptual foundation is built upon a synthesis of ancient wisdom traditions, including Gnosticism, Neoplatonism, Hinduism, Buddhism, and Western occultism. But the modern Theosophical movement most closely associated with Helena Petrovna Blavatsky (1831-1891), often referred to as Madame Blavatsky.

Madame Blavatsky was born in 1831 in Yekaterinoslav, Russian Empire (now Dnipro, Ukraine), into a noble family. From an early age, she demonstrated a fascination with the mystical and the occult. Blavatsky's extensive travels across Europe, the Middle East, and Asia exposed her to a wide array of spiritual traditions and esoteric knowledge, which she would later integrate into her teachings. In 1875, Blavatsky, along with Henry Steel Olcott (1832-1907), William Quan Judge, and others, founded the Theosophical Society in New York City.

Olcott was an American military officer, journalist, and lawyer. He served as the society's first president and played a crucial role in establishing its organizational structure. Olcott was also instrumental in the society's expansion into India and Sri Lanka, where he worked to revive Buddhism and promote religious tolerance.

The society's primary objectives were to promote the study of comparative religion, philosophy, and science, to investigate the unexplained laws of nature and the powers latent in humanity, and to encourage the practice of universal brotherhood. The society's motto, "There is no religion higher than Truth," encapsulated its ethos.

Blavatsky's most significant contributions to Theosophy came in the form of her writings. Her two major works, *Isis Unveiled* (1877) and *The Secret Doctrine* (1888), became foundational texts for the movement. *Isis Unveiled* critiqued contemporary science and religion, arguing that both had lost touch with the ancient wisdom that once connected humanity with the divine. *The Secret Doctrine* went even further, presenting an esoteric cosmology that integrated Eastern and Western spiritual traditions.

Blavatsky claimed that her works were inspired by the Mahatmas, or spiritual masters, who communicated with her through mystical means. Her writings emphasized the idea of a hidden, spiritual hierarchy guiding the evolution of humanity. She introduced concepts such as karma, reincarnation, and the seven root races—each representing a stage in the spiritual evolution of the human race.

Alfred Percy Sinnett (1840-1921), a British journalist and author, Sinnett became involved in Theosophy in the 1880s and played a key role in popularizing the movement in Europe but it was his book The Occult World (1881) that introduced many Western readers to Theosophy and the existence of the Mahatmas. Sinnett's correspondence with the Mahatmas, particularly the letters from Koot Hoomi and Morya, became central to Theosophical teachings.

Her ideas were met with both enthusiasm and skepticism. While some saw her as a profound spiritual teacher, others dismissed her as a charlatan. Nevertheless, Blavatsky's influence was undeniable, and she played a crucial role in popularizing Eastern spirituality in the West.

Theosophists moved the headquarters of the Theosophical Society to Adyar, near Madras (now Chennai), India, in 1882. This move marked the beginning of the society's deep engagement with Indian spirituality, and it attracted numerous Indian intellectuals and spiritual seekers such as Annie Besant (1847-1933) and Charles Webster Leadbeater (1854-1934).

Besant, born in London in 1847, was a prominent social reformer, feminist, and orator before she became involved with Theosophy. Her early life was marked by her activism in causes such as women's rights, birth control, and labor rights. She was a member of the Fabian Society and worked closely with figures like Charles Bradlaugh, advocating for secularism and social justice. But her encounter with Theosophy in 1889 marked a turning point in her life.

After reading *The Secret Doctrine*, Besant was deeply impressed by Blavatsky's teachings and sought to meet her. She quickly became a dedicated member of the Theosophical Society, and after Blavatsky's death in 1891, she emerged as one of the society's most prominent leaders. Under Besant's leadership, the Theosophical Society expanded its influence globally. Besant was instrumental in promoting the society's teachings, giving lectures, writing extensively, and organizing Theosophical groups around the world. Besant's leadership was characterized by her emphasis on social reform and the application of Theosophical principles to address pressing social issues.

In India, Besant became a prominent advocate for Indian self-rule, aligning herself with the Indian nationalist movement against British imperialism. She believed that Theosophy could serve as a bridge between Eastern and Western cultures, fostering mutual understanding and spiritual growth. Besant's efforts to promote education led to the establishment of the Central Hindu College in Benares (now Varanasi), which later became part of Banaras Hindu University.

Besant's collaboration with Charles Webster Leadbeater led to the discovery and promotion of Jiddu Krishnamurti (1895-1986), a young Indian boy whom they believed to be the World Teacher or Maitreya—a messianic figure prophesied in Theosophical teachings. Krishnamurti was groomed to be the World Teacher, a messianic figure in Theosophical prophecy. However, in 1929, Krishnamurti famously dissolved the Order of the Star, a Theosophical organization created to support his mission, and distanced himself from the movement. He went on to become an independent philosopher and spiritual teacher, emphasizing personal inquiry and the rejection of all religious and ideological systems.

The "Krishnamurti affair," the promotion of Krishnamurti, created significant controversy within the Theosophical Society and eventually led to divisions within the movement. For example, Rudolf Steiner (1861-1925), who was initially involved in the German branch of the Theosophical Society, emphasized the application of spiritual principles to education, agriculture, and the arts. He left the society in 1912 largely due to differences over the role of Krishnamurti and the interpretation of esoteric teachings. Steiner eventually formed his own movement, Anthroposophy.

Despite these doctrinal controversies, Besant's contributions to Theosophy were immense. She helped to shape the movement's social and political engagements, particularly in India, and her writings, including *The Ancient Wisdom* (1897) and *Esoteric Christianity* (1901), remain influential within Theosophical circles. Much of her work was completed in partnership with C.W. Leadbeater.

Leadbeater, born in Stockport, England, in 1854, was a former Anglican priest who became one of the most controversial yet influential figures in the Theosophical Society. Leadbeater's journey into Theosophy also began when he encountered Blavatsky's teachings in the late 1880s. He was particularly drawn to the esoteric aspects of Theosophy and quickly became known for his clairvoyant abilities.

Leadbeater's work within the Theosophical Society was marked by his exploration of occult phenomena and his detailed descriptions of the spiritual planes and the afterlife. His book *The Astral Plane* (1895) became a key text in Theosophical literature, offering a comprehensive account of the astral world—a realm of existence beyond the physical plane.

Leadbeater's teachings often focused on the development of psychic abilities and the importance of spiritual practices such as meditation and visualization. He was deeply involved in the promotion of the Liberal

Catholic Church, a movement within Theosophy that sought to integrate Christian rituals with Theosophical teachings.

However, Leadbeater's career was not without controversy. Accusations of sexual misconduct with young boys led to a scandal within the Theosophical Society, resulting in his temporary resignation in 1906. Despite this, Leadbeater remained a central figure in the movement, particularly through his close association with Annie Besant and their promotion of Jiddu Krishnamurti.

His later works, including *The Masters and the Path* (1925), continued to explore the themes of spiritual evolution and the guidance of the Mahatmas. He remained a controversial yet influential figure until his death in 1934.

The ideas of the Theosophists were echoed in other academic and spiritual disciplines. For example the work of the Jesuit scientist and mystic Teilhard de Chardin (see *The Phenomenon of Man*) seems to echo many of the same beliefs. Emergent scientific discoveries and world events, thus, have to be considered in understanding the movement. Theosophy emerged during a time of significant social, political, and intellectual upheaval.

The late 19th century was marked by the rise of industrialization, the spread of European imperialism, and the questioning of traditional religious and scientific paradigms. Theosophy, with its synthesis of Eastern and Western spiritual traditions, appealed to a growing number of people who were disillusioned with orthodox religion and materialistic science.

In the West, Theosophy attracted intellectuals, artists, and social reformers who were interested in exploring alternative spiritualities and philosophies. The movement's emphasis on universal brotherhood and the unity of all religions resonated with those seeking a more inclusive and holistic worldview.

In India, Theosophy played a significant role in the cultural and political revival of the late 19th and early 20th centuries. The society's engagement with Indian spirituality helped to legitimize and promote indigenous religious traditions at a time when they were under threat from colonialism and Christian missionary efforts. And when Theosophists like Annie Besant became prominent figures in the Indian nationalist movement, advocating for self-rule and the revival of traditional Indian education it popularized the movement.

However, Theosophy was not without its critics. Some viewed the movement as a Western appropriation of Eastern spirituality, while others dismissed its teachings as pseudo-scientific and occultist. The movement's emphasis on esoteric knowledge and secret teachings also led to accusations of elitism and authoritarianism. In Europe and America, it was often associated with the broader occult revival of the late 19th and early 20th centuries.

But Theosophical ideas influenced a wide range of cultural and intellectual movements, from the early New Age movement to the development of modern psychology and the study of comparative religion. Theosophy's emphasis on the unity of all religions and the exploration of hidden spiritual knowledge continues to inspire seekers around the world.

Theosophy continues to be a source of inspiration for those seeking to understand the deeper mysteries of existence. The Theosophical Society remains active, with branches around the world dedicated to the study and dissemination of the teachings of Blavatsky, Besant, and Leadbeater.

Theosophists today continue to explore the intersections of spirituality, science, and social justice, recognizing that the challenges of the modern world—such as environmental degradation, social inequality, and violent global conflict—require solutions that are both spiritually informed and practically effective. And this work aligns nicely with contemporary scholarly work.

For example, contemporary physics and neuroscience have begun to explore areas that resonate with Theosophical ideas, particularly in their treatment of consciousness, the nature of reality, and the interconnectedness of all things. Although Theosophy is a spiritual and philosophical system that integrates Eastern religions, Western esotericism, and mystical experiences, it has long promoted ideas about the unity of existence, the evolution of consciousness, and the deeper, often hidden, aspects of reality.

Quantum physics challenges the classical view of a solid, objective reality, suggesting instead that reality is fundamentally probabilistic and perspectival, dependent on observation. This aligns with Theosophical teachings that assert reality is not merely physical but also includes spiritual and mental dimensions. Theosophy posits that what we perceive as the material world is just one aspect of a much broader, multi-dimensional reality. This holographic view of reality is echoed in the ideas presented by physicists like Werner Heisenberg and Niels Bohr, who, through their work in quantum mechanics, have shown that particles exist in multiple states until observed. This concept of the observer effect in quantum mechanics, where the act of observation can affect the state of a quantum system, parallels Theosophical ideas about consciousness shaping reality. Theosophy maintains that consciousness is not just a byproduct of physical processes but an active force that interacts with and influences the material world.

Quantum entanglement, where particles remain connected across vast distances in ways that seem to transcend the speed of light, also resonates with Theosophical concepts of interconnectedness. Theosophy posits that all life and matter are interconnected through an underlying spiritual essence, a unity that modern physics hints at through non-locality and the holistic nature of quantum systems. The ideas presented in works like Fritjof Capra's *The Tao of Physics* and David Bohm's *Wholeness and the Implicate Order* reflect this growing intersection between scientific and Theosophical thought.

In neuroscience, there has been a welcome shift in how consciousness is understood. Traditional neuroscience has long viewed consciousness as a product of brain activity, but more contemporary theories, such as Integrated Information Theory (IIT) developed by Giulio Tononi, suggest that consciousness might be more foundational than previously thought.

This theory proposes that consciousness could be a *fundamental* aspect of the universe, not just a brain-based phenomenon. This aligns with Theosophical beliefs that consciousness permeates all levels of existence and is not limited to or reducible to the human brain. Similarly, the study of mystical experiences, as discussed in works by scholars like William James in *The Varieties of Religious Experience* and contemporary researchers like Andrew Newberg, shows that these experiences often involve altered brain activity, particularly in areas related to self-awareness and perception.

Theosophy has long emphasized the importance of mystical experiences as a means of accessing deeper truths about the universe, and the scientific study of these experiences lends credibility to the Theosophical idea that the mind is capable of accessing higher states of consciousness beyond ordinary perception. Here, we would also point to work in meditation, lucid dreaming, and a re-emerging academic and even medical interest in psychedelics and para-psychology embodied in work by people like Timothy Leary and Ram Dass in the 1960's.

Work by the philosopher David Chalmers, particularly his exploration of the "hard problem" of consciousness, further aligns with Theosophical thought. Chalmers argues that while neuroscience can explain the mechanisms of the brain, it struggles to explain why and how these processes give rise to subjective experiences—what he refers to as *qualia*. This inquiry into the nature of consciousness challenges the reductionist view that consciousness can be entirely explained by physical processes in the brain.

Chalmers' ideas, particularly in publications such as *The Conscious Mind: In Search of a Fundamental Theory*, echo Theosophical views that consciousness is not reducible to brain activity but is something much larger, perhaps even a primary aspect of the universe itself.

Likewise, in Thomas Nagel's argues in his great essay *"What is it Like to Be a Bat?"* that there are aspects of consciousness that cannot be fully understood from a purely objective, scientific standpoint. He suggests that subjective experience—what it is like to be a particular organism—cannot be captured by the reductionist methods of science.

This resonates with the Theosophical notion that consciousness and spiritual experiences transcend physical explanations and that there are dimensions of reality and mind that science is only beginning to touch upon and perhaps are not even suited to explain. His essay highlights the limitations of an objective Enlightenment-science style approach to understanding consciousness, emphasizing the unique, subjective nature of experience that Theosophy has long acknowledged.

Neuroscience continues to explore the intricate connection between the mind and body, particularly how mental states can influence physical health. Theosophical teachings also stress the interconnectedness of mind, body, perception, and spirit, holding that mental and spiritual well-being directly affect physical health, a notion increasingly supported by research in psychosomatic medicine and the study of the placebo effect. Books like Bruce Lipton's *The Biology of Belief* explore how thoughts and beliefs directly affect our physical reality. The relationship of the mind to the world is not as clear cut as Western science once imagined.

Theosphists work this question by exploring how color, aura, and art are entwined with perception, emotion, and consciousness itself. Annie Besant and C.W. Leadbeater in *Thought-Forms* presented in the following pages discuss how colors and forms seen in the aura reflect, or maybe even produce, the emotional and spiritual states of individuals. They show that auras can be perceived by those with heightened spiritual sensitivity and that they represented the interaction if not identity between the physical and spiritual dimensions. This idea sits surprisingly comfortably with modern studies on synesthesia and the relationship between color and emotion in art

In art, color has often been used to express emotional states and spiritual truths. The idea that art can transcend mere representation and tap into far higher levels of consciousness is central to both Theosophy and abstract art. For example, Wassily Kandinsky, an artist deeply influenced by Theosophical ideas, believed that colors and shapes could evoke specific spiritual experiences, reflecting the notion that art and thinking are deeply interconnected with consciousness. Kandinsky's book *Concerning the Spiritual in Art*, explicates how abstract art can evoke spiritual experiences by bypassing the intellect and speaking directly to the soul. Art is as a medium through which deeper truths about the universe and the self can be communicated.

So as contemporary physics and neuroscience have started to explore areas that echo Theosophical interests, it's important to note that these scientific fields remain grounded in Enlightenment style empirical research and often approach these phenomena from a very different philosophical standpoint than Theosophy. For instance, Theosophy treats consciousness as a foundational, pre-existing aspect of the universe, often associated with the divine. In contrast, most contemporary scientific approaches still treat consciousness as emergent, as epiphenomenal to the brain, even when considering that it could be a fundamental element of nature. Moreover, while Theosophy presents a holistic view of the universe where everything is interconnected and spiritual evolution drives the cosmos, scientific theories like systems biology and ecology explore interconnectedness from a purely physical and empirical perspective, sidestepping spiritual or mystical dimensions.

Theosophy integrates ethics and morality into its worldview, seeing spiritual evolution as tied to moral development. Science, particularly in fields like physics and neuroscience, tends to describe how things work rather than prescribe how they should, although the implications of scientific discoveries often provoke ethical debates. For example, the ethical considerations surrounding artificial intelligence and consciousness, as discussed by scholars like Nick Bostrom in *Superintelligence*, reflect a growing concern about the implications of these scientific advancements.

Theosophy has always positioned itself as a bridge between science and the numina, and its claims and questions remain relevant in today's discussions about the nature of consciousness, the structure of reality, and the potential shape of human futures.

As contemporary science and scholarship continues to push the boundaries of our understanding, people often venture into territories that Theosophy has long explored, albeit from a different angle. As we enter into the Anthropocene, marked as it is by environmental, economic, political and social crises and with no clear solution on the horizon, the ongoing dialogue between science and spirituality, which Theosophy has long championed, is more relevant than ever.

FIG I: MADAME BLAVATSKY

Thought-Forms

FORWARD BY AB

The text of this book is a collaborative effort between Mr. Leadbeater and myself. Portions of it have previously appeared as an article in *Lucifer* (now known as *The Theosophical Review*), but the majority of the content is entirely new. The intricate work of drawing and painting the Thought-Forms observed by Mr. Leadbeater, myself, or both of us together, was undertaken by three talented friends—Mr. John Varley, Mr. Prince, and Miss Macfarlane. We extend our deepest gratitude to each of them. Capturing in the dull colors of this world the vibrant, living light of forms from other realms is a challenging and often underappreciated task; their efforts are deserving of the highest recognition. They needed the brilliance of colored fire but had only the limited pigments of the earth at their disposal.

We are also grateful to Mr. F. Bligh Bond for permitting us to use his essay on Vibration Figures, along with some of his exquisite drawings. Additionally, another friend contributed notes and a few drawings but prefers to remain anonymous. To this unnamed contributor, we also send our sincere thanks.

It is our profound hope—and firm belief—that this book will impart a powerful moral lesson to every reader, helping them to understand the nature and influence of their thoughts. We hope it will serve as a catalyst for noble thinking and as a deterrent to base impulses. With these aspirations, we send this work out into the world.

ANNIE BESANT

FIG F: OIL PORTRAIT OF ANNIE BESANT

FIG. F2 CW LEADBETTER

THOUGHT-FORMS

Science's perspective on the invisible world has evolved significantly over time.

As knowledge expands, science no longer confines itself to the tangible physical world. Instead, it now explores the unseen forces and matters that lie beyond the reach of conventional instruments. The concept of ether, once a mere hypothesis, has found a more solid footing in scientific discourse. Mesmerism, now referred to as hypnotism, has transitioned from being dismissed as pseudoscience to gaining some acceptance. Similarly, Reichenbach's experiments, once viewed with skepticism, are now met with less outright rejection. The discovery of Röntgen's rays and the subsequent revolution brought about by radium have drastically altered scientific understandings of matter, propelling science closer to the astral plane and beyond the limits of ether.

The distinction between animate and inanimate matter has blurred, revealing the almost mystical powers of magnets and their inexplicable ability to transfer certain forms of disease.

Phenomena such as telepathy, clairvoyance, and movement without physical contact, while still on the fringes of scientific acceptance, are edging closer to recognition.

Science has delved so deeply into nature's mysteries, employing unparalleled ingenuity and patience, that it is beginning to uncover forces and beings from a higher plane of existence, manifesting at the very edge of the physical world. As the physicist approaches the limits of his domain, he encounters glimpses and hints of another realm that interpenetrates his own. He is compelled to speculate on these invisible presences to rationalize undeniable physical phenomena, unwittingly crossing into the astral plane.

One fascinating path from the physical to the astral world is through the study of thought. Western scientists, beginning with the anatomy and physiology of the brain, attempt to build a "sound psychology" upon this foundation. As they venture into the realms of dreams, illusions, and hallucinations, their efforts to create an experimental science capable of classifying and organizing these phenomena inevitably lead them into the astral plane. Dr. Baraduc of Paris, in his research, has nearly breached this barrier, striving to capture images of astro-mental phenomena—what materialists might interpret as mere vibrations in the brain's gray matter—through photography.

It has long been observed that ultraviolet rays can reflect impressions from objects invisible to the naked eye. Clairvoyants have sometimes been vindicated when figures they described as present during sittings, but invisible to ordinary sight, appeared on sensitive photographic plates. It is difficult for an impartial observer to entirely dismiss the evidence presented by reputable individuals based on their repeated experiments. Today, researchers are increasingly focused on capturing images of these subtle forms, developing specialized methods to reproduce them. Among these researchers, Dr. Baraduc has achieved considerable success and has published a volume detailing his findings, complete with reproductions of the photographs he has obtained.

Dr. Baraduc explains that he is exploring the subtle forces by which the soul—defined as the intelligence mediating between body and spirit—expresses itself, seeking to record its movements using a needle and capture its "luminous" yet invisible vibrations on sensitive plates. He takes steps to exclude external influences such as electricity and heat. While we might skip over his experiments in Biometry, which involve measuring life through movement, we can turn our attention to his work in Iconography, where he attempts to capture the impressions of invisible waves, believed to be of the nature of light, in which the soul imprints its own image.

Several of these photographs depict the etheric and magnetic outcomes of physical phenomena, though these are not directly relevant to our current subject. Dr. Baraduc also conducted experiments where he focused intensely on an object, producing an effect on a sensitive plate corresponding to his thought of the object. In one instance, he attempted to project the image of a lady (now deceased) whom he had known, resulting in an impression that matched a drawing he had made of her on her deathbed. He astutely observes that the creation of an object involves projecting an image from the mind and subsequently materializing it, and he sought to investigate the chemical effects of this thought-created picture on silver salts.

One remarkable example involves the outward projection of a force, symbolizing an earnest prayer. Another image shows a prayer producing forms resembling fern fronds, while yet another depicts something akin to rain falling upwards, if such a notion can be allowed. A rippled, oblong mass was generated by three individuals concentrating on their unity in affection. A young boy, grieving over and caressing a dead bird, is surrounded by a flood of curved, interwoven threads, representing his emotional turmoil.

A powerful vortex emerges from a profound sense of sadness.

Examining this intriguing and thought-provoking series, it becomes apparent that these images do not directly capture the thought itself but rather the effects caused by its vibrations on etheric matter. To fully comprehend the results, it is necessary to perceive the thought clairvoyantly. These illustrations are valuable not only for what they reveal but also for what they leave unseen.

It may be beneficial to clearly present some of the natural phenomena that can help make Dr. Baraduc's findings more comprehensible to students. Although his results are inherently imperfect—given that a physical photographic camera and sensitive plates are not ideal tools for astral research—they are nonetheless fascinating and significant. They serve as a bridge between clairvoyant and physical scientific investigations.

At present, researchers outside the Theosophical Society are becoming increasingly interested in the fact that emotional changes manifest as shifts in color within the cloud-like ovoid or aura that surrounds all living beings. Articles on this subject are appearing in publications not affiliated with the Theosophical Society. One medical specialist, Dr. Hooker of Gloucester Place, London, has compiled numerous cases documenting the color changes in the auras of individuals with varying temperaments. Hooker's findings closely align with those observed by clairvoyant theosophists and others, and the general consensus on this matter lends credibility to the phenomenon if judged by the usual standards applied to human testimony.

C.E. Leadbetter's *Man Visible and Invisible* addresses the general topic of the aura. This current volume, authored by Leadbeater his theosophical colleague Annie Besant, aims to further explore this subject. This this study is particularly valuable in vividly illustrating to students the potent and living nature of thought and desire, as well as the influence these forces exert on all those they reach.

THE DIFFICULTY OF REPRESENTATION

We've often heard the phrase "thoughts are things," and many of us believe in the truth of this statement. However, only a few of us have a clear understanding of what exactly a thought is. The goal of this book is to help us better grasp this concept.

There are significant challenges in our way, especially because our understanding of space is confined to three dimensions, and when we attempt to draw something, we effectively reduce it to two dimensions. Even when we depict ordinary three-dimensional objects, our representation is inherently flawed.

For example, if a road crosses the picture, the part in the foreground must be shown as much wider than the part in the background, even though its width remains constant in reality. Similarly, if we draw a house, the right angles at its corners must be depicted as acute or obtuse, but almost never as they truly are. In essence, we don't draw objects as they are but as they appear.

The artist's challenge is to use lines on a flat surface to create an impression that recalls the appearance of a three-dimensional object.

This is possible only because similar objects are already familiar to those who view the picture and accept the suggestion it conveys. A person who has never seen a tree would struggle to understand one even from the most skillful painting. If we add to this difficulty the far more significant challenge of a limitation of consciousness, and imagine showing the picture to a being who only knows two dimensions, we can see how utterly impossible it would be to convey any adequate impression of the landscape as we see it. This exact difficulty, in its most severe form, arises when we try to draw even a simple thought-form.

Most people are confined to a consciousness of three dimensions and have no understanding of the inner world to which thought-forms belong, with all its magnificent light and color. At best, we can only represent a section of the thought-form, and those who have the ability to see the original will inevitably be disappointed with any reproduction. Still, those who currently cannot see anything will gain at least a partial understanding, and while it may be inadequate, it's better than nothing.

All students know that what we call the aura of a person is the outer part of the cloud-like substance of their higher bodies, which interpenetrate each other and extend beyond the limits of the physical body—the smallest of all. They also know that two of these bodies, the mental and desire bodies, are primarily responsible for the appearance of what we call thought-forms. But to ensure clarity for everyone, including those not already familiar with theosophical teachings, a brief review of the main facts is appropriate.

Man, as a thinker, is surrounded by a body made up of countless combinations of the subtle matter from the mental plane. This body's refinement and organization depend on the individual's level of intellectual development. The mental body is incredibly beautiful, with the delicate and rapid motion of its particles giving it the appearance of living, iridescent light. This beauty becomes even more radiant and captivating as a person's intellect evolves, especially when it is focused on pure and lofty ideas.

Every thought generates a set of corresponding vibrations in this body, accompanied by a stunning display of color, similar to the vibrant colors seen in the spray of a waterfall when sunlight hits it, but magnified to an extraordinary degree. Under the influence of these vibrations, the body releases a vibrating portion of itself, shaped by the nature of the vibrations—similar to how sand forms patterns on a disk vibrating to a musical note. This released portion then attracts similar matter from the surrounding atmosphere, forming a thought-form, a pure and simple living entity, filled with intense activity and driven by the idea that created it. If this thought-form is made of finer matter, it will be powerful and energetic, capable of being a potent agent when directed by a strong and steady will. We will delve into the details of such use later.

When a person's energy is directed outward towards external objects of desire or engaged in passionate and emotional activities, this energy operates in a less subtle form of matter than the mental—specifically, in the astral world. This energy forms the desire-body, which is the most prominent part of the aura in an undeveloped person. In a person of a grosser type, the desire-body is made of denser astral matter and has dull colors, with browns, dirty greens, and reds being predominant.

These colors may flash in various ways as the person's passions are stirred. In contrast, a person of a higher type has a desire-body composed of finer astral matter, with colors that are fine and clear, rippling and flashing through it. While the desire-body is less delicate and radiant than the mental body, it is still a beautiful object, and as selfishness is eliminated, all the duller and heavier shades disappear.

This desire, or astral, body gives rise to a second type of entity, similar in general structure to the thought-forms previously described but limited to the astral plane and generated by the mind under the influence of the animal nature.

These entities are created by the activity of the lower mind, which expresses itself through the astral body—known in theosophical terms as Kâma-Manas, or the mind dominated by desire. In this case, vibrations are set up in the desire-body or astral body, and under their influence, the body releases a vibrating portion of itself, shaped, as before, by the nature of the vibrations.

This portion then attracts some of the corresponding elemental essence of the astral world, forming a thought-form with this elemental essence as its body and the desire or passion that generated it as its animating soul. The strength of this thought-form depends on the amount of mental energy combined with the desire or passion that created it. Like those on the mental plane, these are called artificial elementals, and they are the most common, as few thoughts from ordinary people are entirely free from desire, passion, or emotion.

THE TWO EFFECTS OF THOUGHT

Each definite thought produces a double effect—a radiating vibration and a floating form. The thought itself appears first to clairvoyant sight as a vibration in the mental body, and this may be either simple or complex. If the thought itself is absolutely simple, there is only the one rate of vibration, and only one type of mental matter will be strongly affected. The mental body is composed of matter of several degrees of density, which we commonly arrange in classes according to the sub-planes.

Of each of these we have many sub-divisions, and if we typify these by drawing horizontal lines to indicate the different degrees of density, there is another arrangement which we might symbolize by drawing perpendicular lines at right angles to the others, to denote types which differ in quality as well as in density.

There are thus many varieties of this mental matter, and it is found that each one of these has its own especial and appropriate rate of vibration, to which it seems most accustomed, so that it very readily responds to it, and tends to return to it as soon as possible when it has been forced away from it by some strong rush of thought or feeling.

When a sudden wave of some emotion sweeps over a man, for example, his astral body is thrown into violent agitation, and its original colors are or the time almost obscured by the flush of carmine, of blue, or of scarlet which corresponds with the rate of vibration of that particular emotion.

This change is only temporary; it passes off in a few seconds, and the astral body rapidly resumes its usual condition. Yet every such rush of feeling produces a permanent effect: it always adds a little of its hue to the normal coloring of the astral body, so that every time that the man yields himself to a certain emotion it becomes easier for him to yield himself to it again, because his astral body is getting into the habit of vibrating at that especial rate.

The majority of human thoughts, however, are by no means simple. Absolutely pure affection of course exists; but we very often find it tinged with pride or with selfishness, with jealousy or with animal passion. This means that at least two separate vibrations appear both in the mental and astral bodies—frequently more than two. The radiating vibration, therefore, will be a complex one, and the resultant thought-form will show several colors instead of only one.

HOW THE VIBRATION ACTS

These radiating vibrations, like all others in nature, become less powerful in proportion to the distance from their source, though it is probable that the variation is in proportion to the cube of the distance instead of to the square, because of the additional dimension involved. Again, like all other vibrations, these tend to reproduce themselves whenever opportunity is offered to them; and so whenever they strike upon another mental body they tend to provoke in it their own rate of motion.

That is—from the point of view of the man whose mental body is touched by these waves—they tend to produce in his mind thoughts of the same type as that which had previously arisen in the mind of the thinker who sent forth the waves. The distance to which such thought-waves penetrate, and the force and persistency with which they impinge upon the mental bodies of others, depend upon the strength and clearness of the original thought. In this way the thinker is in the same position as the speaker.

The voice of the latter sets in motion waves of sound in the air which radiate from him in all directions, and convey his message to all those who are within hearing, and the distance to which his voice can penetrate depends upon its power and upon the clearness of his enunciation.

In just the same way the forceful thought will carry very much further than the weak and undecided thought; but clearness and definiteness are of even greater importance than strength. Again, just as the speaker's voice may fall upon heedless ears where men are already engaged in business or in pleasure, so may a mighty wave of thought sweep past without affecting the mind of the man, if he be already deeply engrossed in some other line of thought.

It should be understood that this radiating vibration conveys the character of the thought, but not its subject. If a Hindu sits rapt in devotion to Kṛiṣhṇa, the waves of feeling which pour forth from him stimulate devotional feeling in all those who come under their influence, though in the case of the Muhammadan that devotion is to Allah, while for the Zoroastrian it is to Ahuramazda, or for the Christian to Jesus.

A man thinking keenly upon some high subject pours out from himself vibrations which tend to stir up thought at a similar level in others, but they in no way suggest to those others the special subject of his thought. They naturally act with special vigor upon those minds already habituated to vibrations of similar character; yet they have some effect on every mental body upon which they impinge, so that their tendency is to awaken the power of higher thought in those to whom it has not yet become a custom.

It is thus evident that every man who thinks along high lines is doing missionary work, even though he may be entirely unconscious of it.

THE FORM AND ITS EFFECT

Let us turn now to the second effect of thought, the creation of a definite form. All students of the occult are acquainted with the idea of the elemental essence, that strange half-intelligent life which surrounds us in all directions, vivifying the matter of the mental and astral planes. This matter thus animated responds very readily to the influence of human thought, and every impulse sent out, either from the mental body or from the astral body of man, immediately clothes itself in a temporary vehicle of this vitalized matter.

Such a thought or impulse becomes for the time a kind of living creature, the thought-force being the soul, and the vivified matter the body. Instead of using the somewhat clumsy paraphrase, "astral or mental matter ensouled by the monadic essence at the stage of one of the elemental kingdoms," theosophical writers often, for brevity's sake, call this quickened matter simply elemental essence; and sometimes they speak of the thought-form as "an elemental."

There may be infinite variety in the color and shape of such elementals or thought-forms, for each thought draws round it the matter which is appropriate for its expression, and sets that matter into vibration in harmony with its own; so that the character of the thought decides its color, and the study of its variations and combinations is an exceedingly interesting one.

This thought-form may not inaptly be compared to a Leyden jar, the coating of living essence being symbolized by the jar, and the thought energy by the charge of electricity.

If the man's thought or feeling is directly connected with someone else, the resultant thought-form moves towards that person and discharges itself upon his astral and mental bodies. If the man's thought is about himself, or is based upon a personal feeling, as the vast majority of thoughts are, it hovers round its creator and is always ready to react upon him whenever he is for a moment in a passive condition. For example, a man who yields himself to thoughts of impurity may forget all about them while he is engaged in the daily routine of his business, even though the resultant forms are hanging round him in a heavy cloud, because his attention is otherwise directed and his astral body is therefore not impressible by any other rate of vibration than its own.

When, however, the marked vibration slackens and the man rests after his labours and leaves his mind blank as regards definite thought, he is very likely to feel the vibration of impurity stealing insidiously upon him. If the consciousness of the man be to any extent awakened, he may perceive this and cry out that he is being tempted by the devil; yet the truth is that the temptation is from without only in appearance, since it is nothing but the natural reaction upon him of his own thought-forms.

Each man travels through space enclosed within a cage of his own building, surrounded by a mass of the forms created by his habitual thoughts. Through this medium he looks out upon the world, and naturally he sees everything tinged with its predominant colors, and all rates of vibration which reach him from without are more or less modified by its rate. Thus until the man learns complete control of thought and feeling, he sees nothing as it really is, since all his observations must be made through this medium, which distorts and colours everything like badly-made glass.

If the thought-form be neither definitely personal nor specially aimed at someone else, it simply floats detached in the atmosphere, all the time radiating vibrations similar to those originally sent forth by its creator.

If it does not come into contact with any other mental body, this radiation gradually exhausts its store of energy, and in that case the form falls to pieces; but if it succeeds in awakening sympathetic vibration in any mental body near at hand, an attraction is set up, and the thought-form is usually absorbed by that mental body.

Thus we see that the influence of the thought-form is by no means so far-reaching as that of the original vibration; but in so far as it acts, it acts with much greater precision. What it produces in the mind-body which it influences is not merely a thought of an order similar to that which gave it birth; it is actually the same thought.

The radiation may affect thousands and stir up in them thoughts on the same level as the original, and yet it may happen that no one of them will be identical with that original; the thought-form can affect only very few, but in those few cases it will reproduce exactly the initiatory idea.

The fact of the creation by vibrations of a distinct form, geometrical or other, is already familiar to every student of acoustics, and "Chladni's" figures are continually reproduced in every physical laboratory.

FIG 1. *CHLADNI PLATE*

2 NODAL LINES

FIG

FIG. 3. FORMS PRODUCED IN SOUND.

German physicist and musician Ernst Chladni (1756–1827) experimented with vibrating plates and nodal patterns. More than a century earlier the English scientist Robert Hooke had run a violin bow along the edge of a flour-covered glass plate and observed strange patterns forming. These patterns were caused by "nodal lines" (the still areas of an otherwise vibrating plate). Chladni perfected Hooke's initial experiments and decribed them in *Entdeckungen über die Theorie des*

Klanges (*Discoveries in the Theory of Sound, 1787*). These patterns are now commonly termed "Chladni figures."

For the lay reader the following brief description may be useful. A Chladni's sound plate (fig. 1) is made of brass or plate-glass.

Grains of fine sand or spores are scattered over the surface, and the edge of the plate is bowed. The sand is thrown up into the air by the vibration of the plate, and re-falling on the plate is arranged in regular lines (fig. 2).

By touching the edge of the plate at different points when it is bowed, different notes, and hence varying forms, are obtained (fig. 3). If the figures here given are compared with those obtained from the human voice, many likenesses will be observed. For these latter, the 'voice-forms' so admirably studied and pictured by Mrs Watts Hughes (See *Eidophone Voice Figures)* bearing witness to the same fact, should be consulted, and her work on the subject should be in the hands of every student.

But few perhaps have realized that the shapes pictured are due to the interplay of the vibrations that create them, and that a machine exists by means of which two or more simultaneous motions can be imparted to a pendulum, and that by attaching a fine drawing-pen to a lever connected with the pendulum its action may be exactly traced.

Substitute for the swing of the pendulum the vibrations set up in the mental or astral body, and we have clearly before us the modus operandi of the building of forms by vibrations. (Mr Joseph Gould of Stratford House, Nottingham, supplies the twin-elliptic pendulum by which these wonderful figures may be produced).

The following description is taken from a most interesting essay entitled *Vibration Figures*, by F. Bligh Bond, F.R.I.B.A., who has drawn a number of remarkable figures by the use of pendulums. The pendulum is suspended on knife edges of hardened steel, and is free to swing only at right angles to the knife-edge suspension.

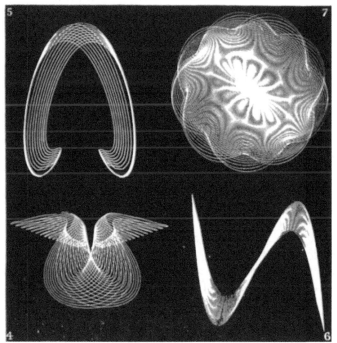

4-7 FORMS PRODUCED BY PENDULUMS

Four such pendulums may be coupled in pairs, swinging at right angles to each other, by threads connecting the shafts of each pair of pendulums with the ends of a light but rigid lath, from the center of which run other threads; these threads carry the united movements of each pair of pendulums to a light square of wood, suspended by a spring, and bearing a pen.

The pen is thus controlled by the combined movement of the four pendulums, and this movement is registered on a drawing board by the pen. There is no limit, theoretically, to the number of pendulums that can be combined in this manner.

The movements are rectilinear, but two rectilinear vibrations of equal amplitude acting at right angles to each other generate a circle if they alternate precisely, an ellipse if the alternations are less regular or the amplitudes unequal.

A cyclic vibration may also be obtained from a pendulum free to swing in a rotary path. In these ways a most wonderful series of drawings have been obtained, and the similarity of these to some of the thought-forms is remarkable; they suffice to demonstrate how readily vibrations may be transformed into figures.

Thus compare fig. 4 with fig. 12, the mother's prayer; or fig. 5 with fig. 10; or fig. 6 with fig. 25, the serpent-like darting forms. Fig. 7 is added as an illustration of the complexity attainable. It seems to us a most marvelous thing that some of the drawings, made apparently at random by the use of this machine, should exactly correspond to higher types of thought-forms created in meditation.

We are sure that a wealth of significance lies behind this fact, though it will need much further investigation before we can say certainly all that it means. But it must surely imply this much—that, if two forces on the physical plane bearing a certain ratio one to the other can draw a form which exactly corresponds to that produced on the mental plane by a complex thought, we may infer that that thought sets in motion on its own plane two forces which are in the same ratio one to the other. What these forces are and how they work remains to be seen; but if we are ever able to solve this problem, it is likely that it will open to us a new and exceedingly valuable field of knowledge.

FIG. FE 21ST CENTURY RESEARCH ON CHAOS THEORY

The movement of the double pendulum operates as a critique of Enlightenment style emphasis on rationality and the belief in a fully predictable, orderly universe governed by deterministic laws. While Enlightenment science championed the idea that with enough knowledge, everything could be understood and predicted, the chaotic behavior of the double pendulum reveals limitations of this perspective. It shows that even in a system governed by clear physical laws, outcomes can be wildly unpredictable, challenging the notion that rationality alone can fully explain or control anything in the natural world. This unpredictability suggests that the complexity of reality defies linear understanding. This work also holds significant implications for our understanding of time, insofar as it may be plural but irreversible.

GENERAL PRINCIPLES OF THOUGHT-FORMS

Three general principles underlie the production of all thought-forms:—

1. Quality of thought determines color.

2. Nature of thought determines form.

3. Definiteness of thought determines clearness of outline.

THE MEANING OF THE COLOURS

The table of colours given in the frontispiece has already been thoroughly described in the book *Man Visible and Invisible*, and the meaning to be attached to them is just the same in the thought-form as in the body out of which it is evolved.

For the sake of those who have not at hand the full description given in the book just mentioned, it will be well to state that black means hatred and malice. Red, of all shades from lurid brick-red to brilliant scarlet, indicates anger; brutal anger will show as flashes of lurid red from dark brown clouds, while the anger of "noble indignation" is a vivid scarlet, by no means unbeautiful, though it gives an unpleasant thrill; a particularly dark and unpleasant red, almost exactly the color called dragon's blood, shows animal passion and sensual desire of various kinds.

Clear brown (almost burnt sienna) shows avarice; hard dull brown-grey is a sign of selfishness—a color which is indeed painfully common; deep heavy grey signifies depression, while a livid pale grey is associated with fear; grey-green is a signal of deceit, while brownish-green (usually flecked with points and flashes of scarlet) betokens jealousy.

Green seems always to denote adaptability; in the lowest case, when mingled with selfishness, this adaptability becomes deceit; at a later stage, when the color becomes purer, it means rather the wish to be all things to all men, even though it may be chiefly for the sake of becoming popular and bearing a good reputation with them; in its still higher, more delicate and more luminous aspect, it shows the divine power of sympathy.

Affection expresses itself in all shades of crimson and rose; a full clear carmine means a strong healthy affection of normal type; if stained heavily with brown-grey, a selfish and grasping feeling is indicated, while pure pale rose marks that absolutely unselfish love which is possible only to high natures; it passes from the dull crimson of animal love to the most exquisite shades of delicate rose, like the early flushes of the dawning, as the love becomes purified from all selfish elements, and flows out in wider and wider circles of generous impersonal tenderness and compassion to all who are in need. With a touch of the blue of devotion in it, this may express a strong realization of the universal brotherhood of humanity.

Deep orange imports pride or ambition, and the various shades of yellow denote intellect or intellectual gratification, dull yellow ochre implying the direction of such faculty to selfish purposes, while clear gamboge shows a distinctly higher type, and pale luminous primrose yellow is a sign of the highest and most unselfish use of intellectual power, the pure reason directed to spiritual ends.

The different shades of blue all indicate religious feeling, and range through all hues from the dark brown-blue of selfish devotion, or the pallid grey-blue of fetish-worship tinged with fear, up to the rich deep clear color of heartfelt adoration, and the beautiful pale azure of that highest form which implies self-renunciation and union with the divine; the devotional thought of an unselfish heart is very lovely in color, like the deep blue of a summer sky. Through such clouds of blue will often shine out golden stars of great brilliancy, darting upwards like a shower of sparks.

A mixture of affection and devotion is manifested by a tint of violet, and the more delicate shades of this invariably show the capacity of absorbing and responding to a high and beautiful ideal. The brilliancy and the depth of the colors are usually a measure of the strength and the activity of the feeling. Another consideration which must not be forgotten is the type of matter in which these forms are generated. If a thought be purely intellectual and impersonal—for example, if the thinker is attempting to solve a problem in algebra or geometry—the thought-form and the wave of vibration will be confined entirely to the mental plane.

If, however, the thought be of a spiritual nature, if it be tinged with love and aspiration or deep unselfish feeling, it will rise upwards from the mental plane and will borrow much of the splendor and glory of the buddhic level. In such a case its influence is exceedingly powerful, and every such thought is a mighty force for good which cannot but produce a decided effect upon all mental bodies within reach, if they contain any quality at all capable of response.

If, on the other hand, the thought has in it something of self or of personal desire, at once its vibration turns downwards, and it draws round itself a body of astral matter in addition to its clothing of mental matter. Such a thought-form is capable of acting upon the astral bodies of other men as well as their minds, so that it cannot only raise thought within them, but can also stir up their feelings.

THREE CLASSES OF THOUGHT-FORMS

From the point of view of the forms which they produce we may group thought into three classes:—

First, That which takes the image of the thinker. When a man thinks of himself as in some distant place, or wishes earnestly to be in that place, he makes a thought-form in his own image which appears there. Such a form has not infrequently been seen by others, and has sometimes been taken for the astral body or apparition of the man himself. In such a case, either the seer must have enough of clairvoyance for the time to be able to observe that astral shape, or the thought-form must have sufficient strength to materialize itself—that is, to draw round itself temporarily a certain amount of physical matter.

The thought which generates such a form as this must necessarily be a strong one, and it therefore employs a larger proportion of the matter of the mental body, so that though the form is small and compressed when it leaves the thinker, it draws round it a considerable amount of astral matter, and usually expands to life-size before it appears at its destination.

Second, that which takes the image of some material object. When a man thinks of his friend he forms within his mental body a minute image of that friend, which often passes outward and usually floats suspended in the air before him. In the same way if he thinks of a room, a house, a landscape, tiny images of these things are formed within the mental body and afterwards externalized.

This is equally true when he is exercising his imagination; the painter who forms a conception of his future picture builds it up out of the matter of his mental body, and then projects it into space in front of him, keeps it before his mind's eye, and copies it. The novelist in the same way builds images of his character in mental matter, and by the exercise of his will moves these puppets from one position or grouping to another, so that the plot of his story is literally acted out before him.

With our curiously inverted conceptions of reality it is hard for us to understand that these mental images actually exist, and are so entirely objective that they may readily be seen by the clairvoyant, and can even be rearranged by some one other than their creator. Some novelists have been dimly aware of such a process, and have testified that their characters when once created developed a will of their own, and insisted on carrying the plot of the story along lines quite different from those originally intended by the author.

This has happened, sometimes because the thought-forms were ensouled by playful nature-spirits, or more often because some 'dead' novelist, watching on the astral plane the development of the plan of his fellow-author, thought that he could improve upon it, and chose this method of putting forward his suggestions.

Third, that which takes a form entirely its own, expressing its inherent qualities in the matter which it draws round it. Only thought-forms of this third class can usefully be illustrated, for to represent those of the first or second class would be merely to draw portraits or landscapes. In those types we have the plastic mental or astral matter molded in imitation of forms belonging to the physical plane; in this third group we have a glimpse of the forms natural to the astral or mental planes. Yet this very fact, which makes them so interesting, places an insuperable barrier in the way of their accurate reproduction.

Thought-forms of this third class almost invariably manifest themselves upon the astral plane, as the vast majority of them are expressions of feeling as well as of thought. Those of which we here give specimens are almost wholly of that class, except that we take a few examples of the beautiful thought-forms created in definite meditation by those who, through long practice, have learnt how to think.

Thought-forms directed towards individuals produce definitely marked effects, these effects being either partially reproduced in the aura of the recipient and so increasing the total result, or repelled from it.

A thought of love and of desire to protect, directed strongly towards some beloved object, creates a form which goes to the person thought of, and remains in his aura as a shielding and protecting agent; it will seek all opportunities to serve, and all opportunities to defend, not by a conscious and deliberate action, but by a blind following out of the impulse impressed upon it, and it will strengthen friendly forces that impinge on the aura and weaken unfriendly ones. Thus may we create and maintain veritable guardian angels round those we love, and many a mother's prayer for a distant child thus circles round him, though she knows not the method by which her "prayer is answered."

In cases in which good or evil thoughts are projected at individuals, those thoughts, if they are to directly fulfil their mission, must find, in the aura of the object to whom they are sent, materials capable of responding sympathetically to their vibrations.

Any combination of matter can only vibrate within certain definite limits, and if the thought-form be outside all the limits within which the aura is capable of vibrating, it cannot affect that aura at all. It consequently rebounds from it, and that with a force proportionate to the energy with which it impinged upon it.

This is why it is said that a pure heart and mind are the best protectors against any inimical assaults, for such a pure heart and mind will construct an astral and a mental body of fine and subtle materials, and these bodies cannot respond to vibrations that demand coarse and dense matter.

If an evil thought, projected with malefic intent, strikes such a body, it can only rebound from it, and it is flung back with all its own energy; it then flies backward along the magnetic line of least resistance, that which it has just traversed, and strikes its projector; he, having matter in his astral and mental bodies similar to that of the thought-form he generated, is thrown into respondent vibrations, and suffers the destructive effects he had intended to cause to another.

Thus "curses [and blessings] come home to roost." From this arise also the very serious effects of hating or suspecting a good and highly-advanced man; the thought-forms sent against him cannot injure him, and they rebound against their projectors, shattering them mentally, morally, or physically.

Several such instances are well known to members of the Theosophical Society, having come under their direct observation.

So long as any of the coarser kinds of matter connected with evil and selfish thoughts remain in a person's body, he is open to attack from those who wish him evil, but when he has perfectly eliminated these by self-purification his haters cannot injure him, and he goes on calmly and peacefully amid all the darts of their malice. But it is bad for those who shoot out such darts.

Another point that should be mentioned before passing to the consideration of our illustrations is that every one of the thought-forms here given is drawn from life. They are not imaginary forms, prepared as some dreamer thinks that they ought to appear; they are representations of forms actually observed as thrown off by ordinary men and women, and either reproduced with all possible care and fidelity by those who have seen them, or with the help of artists to whom the seers have described them.

For convenience of comparison thought-forms of a similar kind are grouped together in the forthcoming pages.

ILLUSTRATIVE THOUGHT-FORMS

AFFECTION

Vague Pure Affection.—Fig. 8 is a revolving cloud of pure affection, and except for its vagueness it represents a very good feeling. The person from whom it emanates is happy and at peace with the world, thinking dreamily of some friend whose very presence is a pleasure. There is nothing keen or strong about the feeling, yet it is one of gentle well-being, and of an unselfish delight in the proximity of those who are beloved. The feeling which gives birth to such a cloud is pure of its kind, but there is in it no force capable of producing definite results.

An appearance by no means unlike this frequently surrounds a gently purring cat, and radiates slowly outward from the animal in a series of gradually enlarging concentric shells of rosy cloud, fading into invisibility at a distance of a few feet from their drowsily contented creator.

Vague Selfish Affection.—Fig. 9 shows us also a cloud of affection, but this time it is deeply tinged with a far less desirable feeling. The dull hard brown-grey of selfishness shows itself very decidedly among the carmine of love, and thus we see that the affection which is indicated is closely connected with satisfaction at favors already received, and with a lively anticipation of others to come in the near future.

Indefinite as was the feeling which produced the cloud in Fig. 8, it was at least free from this taint of selfishness, and it therefore showed a certain nobility of nature in its author. Fig. 9 represents what takes the place of that condition of mind at a lower level of evolution. It would scarcely be possible that these two clouds should emanate from the same person in the same incarnation. Yet there is good in the man who generates this second cloud, though as yet it is but partially evolved. A vast amount of the average affection of the world is of this type, and it is only by slow degrees that it develops towards the other and higher manifestation.

Definite Affection.—Even the first glance at Fig. 10 shows us that here we have to deal with something of an entirely different nature—something effective and capable, something that will achieve a result.

The color is fully equal to that of Fig. 8 in clearness and depth and transparency, but what was there a mere sentiment is in this case translated into emphatic intention coupled with unhesitating action.

Those who have seen the book *Man Visible and Invisible* will recollect that in Plate XI. of that volume is depicted the effect of a sudden rush of pure unselfish affection as it showed itself in the astral body of a mother, as she caught up her little child and covered it with kisses.

Various changes resulted from that sudden outburst of emotion; one of them was the formation within the astral body of large crimson coils or vortices lined with living light. Each of these is a thought-form of intense affection generated as we have described, and almost instantaneously ejected towards the object of the feeling. Fig. 10 depicts just such a thought-form after it has left the astral body of its author, and is on its way towards its goal.

It will be observed that the almost circular form has changed into one somewhat resembling a projectile or the head of a comet; and it will be easily understood that this alteration is caused by its rapid forward motion.

The clearness of the color assures us of the purity of the emotion which gave birth to this thought-form, while the precision of its outline is unmistakable evidence of power and of vigorous purpose. The soul that gave birth to a thought-form such as this must already be one of a certain amount of development.

Radiating Affection.—Fig. 11 gives us our first example of a thought-form intentionally generated, since its author is making the effort to pour himself forth in love to all beings.

It must be remembered that all these forms are in constant motion. This one, for example, is steadily widening out, though there seems to be an exhaustless fountain welling up through the center from a dimension which we cannot represent.

A sentiment such as this is so wide in its application, that it is very difficult for anyone not thoroughly trained to keep it clear and precise. The thought-form here shown is, therefore, a very creditable one, for it will be noted that all the numerous rays of the star are commendably free from vagueness.

RADIATING AFFECTION.—FIG. 11

Peace and Protection.—Few thought-forms are more beautiful and expressive than this which we see in Fig. 12. This is a thought of love and peace, protection and benediction, sent forth by one who has the power and has earned the right to bless.

It is not at all probable that in the mind of its creator there existed any thought of its beautiful wing-like shape, though it is possible that some unconscious reflection of far-away lessons of childhood about guardian angels who always hovered over their charges may have had its influence in determining this.

However that may be, the earnest wish undoubtedly clothed itself in this graceful and expressive outline, while the affection that prompted it gave to it its lovely rose-color, and the intellect which guided it shone forth like sunlight as its heart and central support.

Thus, in sober truth we may make veritable guardian angels to hover over and protect those whom we love, and many an unselfish earnest wish for good produces such a form as this, though all unknown to its creator.

Grasping Animal Affection.—Fig. 13 gives us an instance of grasping animal affection—if indeed such a feeling as this be deemed worthy of the august name of affection at all.

Several colors bear their share in the production of its dull unpleasing hue, tinged as it is with the lurid gleam of sensuality, as well as deadened with the heavy tint indicative of selfishness.

Especially characteristic is its form, for those curving hooks are never seen except when there exists a strong craving for personal possession.

It is regrettably evident that the fabricator of this thought-form had no conception of the self-sacrificing love which pours itself out in joyous service, never once thinking of result or return; his thought has been, not "How much can I give?" but "How much can I gain?" and so it has expressed itself in these re-entering curves.

It has not even ventured to throw itself boldly outward, as do other thoughts, but projects half-heartedly from the astral body, which must be supposed to be on the left of the picture.

A sad travesty of the divine quality love; yet even this is a stage in evolution, and distinctly an improvement upon earlier stages, as will presently be seen.

DEVOTION

Vague Religious Feeling.—Fig. 14 shows us another shapeless rolling cloud, but this time it is blue instead of crimson. It betokens that vaguely pleasurable religious feeling—a sensation of devoutness rather than of devotion—which is so common among those in whom piety is more developed than intellect.

In many a church one may see a great cloud of deep dull blue floating over the heads of the congregation—

indefinite in outline, because of the indistinct nature of the thoughts and feelings which cause it; flecked too often with brown and grey, because ignorant devotion absorbs with deplorable facility the dismal tincture of selfishness or fear; but none the less adumbrating a mighty potentiality of the future, manifesting to our eyes the first faint flutter of one at least of the twin wings of devotion and wisdom, by the use of which the soul flies upward to God from whom it came.

Strange is it to note under what varied circumstances this vague blue cloud may be seen; and oftentimes its absence speaks more loudly than its presence. For in many a fashionable place of worship we seek it in vain, and find instead of it a vast conglomeration of thought-forms of that second type which take the shape of material objects.

Instead of tokens of devotion, we see floating above the "worshippers" the astral images of hats and bonnets, of jewelry and gorgeous dresses, of horses and of carriages, of whisky-bottles and of Sunday dinners, and sometimes of whole rows of intricate calculations, showing that men and women alike have had during their supposed hours of prayer and praise no thoughts but of business or of pleasure, of the desires or the anxieties of the lower form of mundane existence.

Yet sometimes in a humbler fane, in a church belonging to the unfashionable Catholic or Ritualist, or even in a lowly meeting-house where there is but little of learning or of culture, one may watch the deep blue clouds rolling ceaselessly eastward towards the altar, or upwards, testifying at least to the earnestness and the reverence of those who give them birth.

Rarely—very rarely—among the clouds of blue will flash like a lance cast by the hand of a giant such a thought-form as is shown in Fig. 15; or such a flower of self-renunciation as we see in Fig. 16 may float before our ravished eyes; but in most cases we must seek elsewhere for these signs of a higher development.

Upward Rush of Devotion.—The form in Fig. 15 bears much the same relation to that of Fig. 14 as did the clearly outlined projectile of Fig. 10 to the indeterminate cloud of Fig. 8.

We could hardly have a more marked contrast than that between the inchoate flaccidity of the nebulosity in Fig. 14 and the virile vigor of the splendid spire of highly developed devotion which leaps into being before us in Fig. 15.

This is no uncertain half-formed sentiment; it is the outrush into manifestation of a grand emotion rooted deep in the knowledge of fact.

The man who feels such devotion as this is one who knows in whom he has believed; the man who makes such a thought-form as this is one who has taught himself how to think.

The determination of the upward rush points to courage as well as conviction, while the sharpness of its outline shows the clarity of its creator's conception, and the peerless purity of its color bears witness to his utter unselfishness.

The Response to Devotion.—In Fig. 17 we see the result of his thought—the response of the Logos to the appeal made to Him, the truth which underlies the highest and best part of the persistent belief in an answer to prayer. It needs a few words of explanation. On every plane of His solar system our Logos pours forth His light, His power, His life, and naturally it is on the higher planes that this outpouring of divine strength can be given most fully.

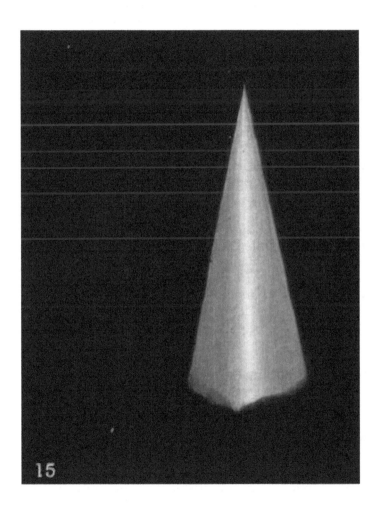

The descent from each plane to that next below it means an almost paralysing limitation—a limitation entirely incomprehensible except to those who have experienced the higher possibilities of human consciousness.

Thus the divine life flows forth with incomparably greater fulness on the mental plane than on the astral; and yet even its glory at the mental level is ineffably transcended by that of the buddhic plane.

Normally each of these mighty waves of influence spreads about its appropriate plane—horizontally, as it were—but it does not pass into the obscuration of a plane lower than that for which it was originally intended.

Yet there are conditions under which the grace and strength peculiar to a higher plane may in a measure be brought down to a lower one, and may spread abroad there with wonderful effect. This seems to be possible when a special channel is for the moment opened; and that work must be done from below and by the effort of man.

It has before been explained that whenever a man's thought or feeling is selfish, the energy which it produces moves in a close curve, and thus inevitably returns and expends itself upon its own level.

But when the thought or feeling is absolutely unselfish, its energy rushes forth in an open curve, and thus does not return in the ordinary sense, but pierces through into the plane above, because only in that higher condition, with its additional dimension, can it find room for its expansion.

But in thus breaking through, such a thought or feeling holds open a door (to speak symbolically) of dimension equivalent to its own diameter, and thus furnishes the requisite channel through which the divine force appropriate to the higher plane can pour itself into the lower with marvelous results, not only for the thinker but for others. An attempt is made in Fig. 17 to symbolize this, and to indicate the great truth that an infinite flood of the higher type of force is always ready and waiting to pour through when the channel is offered, just as the water in a cistern may be said to be waiting to pour through the first pipe that may be opened.

The result of the descent of divine life is a very great strengthening and uplifting of the maker of the channel, and the spreading all about him of a most powerful and beneficent influence. This effect has often been called an answer to prayer, and has been attributed by the ignorant to what they call a "special interposition of Providence," instead of to the unerring action of the great and immutable divine law.

Self-Renunciation.—Fig. 16 gives us yet another form of devotion, producing an exquisitely beautiful form of a type quite new to us—a type in which one might at first sight suppose that various graceful shapes belonging to animate nature were being imitated.

Fig. 16, for example, is somewhat suggestive of a partially opened flower-bud, while other forms are found to bear a certain resemblance to shells or leaves or tree-shapes. Manifestly, however, these are not and cannot be copies of vegetable or animal forms, and it seems probable that the explanation of the similarity lies very much deeper than that. An analogous and even more significant fact is that some very complex thought-forms can be exactly imitated by the action of certain mechanical forces, as has been said above.

While with our present knowledge it would be unwise to attempt a solution of the very fascinating problem presented by these remarkable resemblances, it seems likely that we are obtaining a glimpse across the threshold of a very mighty mystery, for if by certain thoughts we produce a form which has been duplicated by the processes of nature, we have at least a presumption that these forces of nature work along lines somewhat similar to the action of those thoughts.

Since the universe is itself a mighty thought-form called into existence by the Logos, it may well be that tiny parts of it are also the thought-forms of minor entities engaged in the same work; and thus perhaps we may approach a comprehension of what is meant by the three hundred and thirty million Devas of the Hindus.

This form is of the loveliest pale azure, with a glory of white light shining through it—something indeed to tax the skill even of the indefatigable artist who worked so hard to get them as nearly right as possible.

It is what a Catholic would call a definite "act of devotion"—better still, an act of utter selflessness, of self-surrender and renunciation.

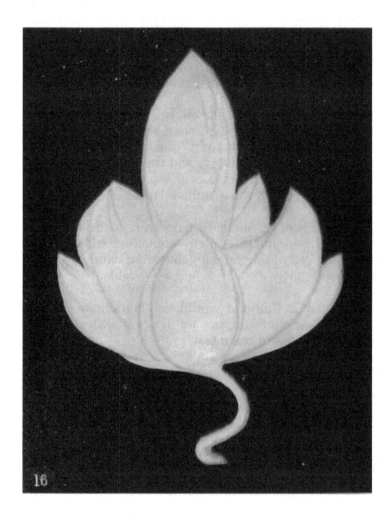

INTELLECT

Vague Intellectual Pleasure.—Fig. 18 represents a vague cloud of the same order as those shown in Figs. 8 and 14, but in this case the colour is yellow instead of crimson or blue. Yellow in any of man's vehicles always indicates intellectual capacity, but its shades vary very much, and it may be complicated by the admixture of other hues.

Generally speaking, it has a deeper and duller tint if the intellect is directed chiefly into lower channels, more especially if the objects are selfish. In the astral or mental body of the average man of business it would show itself as yellow ochre, while pure intellect devoted to the study of philosophy or mathematics appears frequently to be golden, and this rises gradually to a beautiful clear and luminous lemon or primrose yellow when a powerful intellect is being employed absolutely unselfishly for the benefit of humanity.

Most yellow thought-forms are clearly outlined, and a vague cloud of this color is comparatively rare. It indicates intellectual pleasure—appreciation of the result of ingenuity, or the delight felt in clever workmanship. Such pleasure as the ordinary man derives from the contemplation of a picture usually depends chiefly upon the emotions of admiration, affection, or pity which it arouses within him, or sometimes, if it portrays a scene with which he is familiar, its charm consists in its power to awaken the memory of past joys.

An artist, however, may derive from a picture a pleasure of an entirely different character, based upon his recognition of the excellence of the work, and of the ingenuity which has been exercised in producing certain results. Such pure intellectual gratification shows itself in a yellow cloud; and the same effect may be produced by delight in musical ingenuity, or the subtleties of argument. A cloud of this nature betokens the absence of any personal emotion, for if that were present it would inevitably tinge the yellow with its own appropriate color.

FIG. 18. VAGUE INTELLECTUAL PLEASURE

The Intention to Know.—Fig. 19 is of interest as showing us something of the growth of a thought-form. The earlier stage, which is indicated by the upper form, is not uncommon, and indicates the determination to solve some problem—the intention to know and to understand. Sometimes a theosophical lecturer sees many of these yellow serpentine forms projecting towards him from his audience, and welcomes them as a token that his hearers are following his arguments intelligently, and have an earnest desire to understand and to know more.

A form of this kind frequently accompanies a question, and if, as is sometimes unfortunately the case, the question is put less with the genuine desire for knowledge than for the purpose of exhibiting the acumen of the questioner, the form is strongly tinged with the deep orange that indicates conceit. It was at a theosophical meeting that this special shape was encountered, and it accompanied a question which showed considerable thought and penetration.

The answer at first given was not thoroughly satisfactory to the inquirer, who seems to have received the impression that his problem was being evaded by the lecturer. His resolution to obtain a full and thorough answer to his inquiry became more determined than ever, and his thought-form deepened in color and changed into the second of the two shapes, resembling a cork-screw even more closely than before.

Forms similar to these are constantly created by ordinary idle and frivolous curiosity, but as there is no intellect involved in that case the color is no longer yellow, but usually closely resembles that of decaying meat, somewhat like that shown in Fig. 29 as expressing a drunken man's craving for alcohol.

High Ambition.—Fig. 20 gives us another manifestation of desire—the ambition for place or power.

The ambitious quality is shown by a deep orange colour, and the desire by the hooked extensions which precede the form. The thought is a good and pure one of its kind, for if there were anything base or selfish in the desire it would inevitably show itself in the darkening of the clear orange hue.

If this man coveted place or power, it was not for his own sake, but from the conviction that he could do the work well and truly, and to the advantage of his fellow-men.

FIG. 19. THE INTENTION TO KNOW

FIG. 20. HIGH AMBITION

High Ambition.—Fig. 20 gives us another manifestation of desire—the ambition for place or power. The ambitious quality is shown by the rich deep orange colour, and the desire by the hooked extensions which precede the form as it moves.

The thought is a good and pure one of its kind, for if there were anything base or selfish in the desire it would inevitably show itself in the darkening of the clear orange hue by dull reds, browns, or greys.

If this man coveted place or power, it was not for his own sake, but from the conviction that he could do the work well and truly, and to the advantage of his fellow-men.

Selfish Ambition.—Ambition of a lower type is represented in Fig. 21. Not only have we here a large stain of the dull brown-grey of selfishness, but there is also a considerable difference in the form, though it appears to possess equal definiteness of outline. Fig. 20 is rising steadily onward towards a definite object, for it will be observed that the central part of it is as definitely a projectile as Fig. 10.

Fig. 21, on the other hand, is a floating form, and is strongly indicative of general acquisitiveness—the ambition to grasp for the self everything that is within sight.

ANGER

Murderous Rage and Sustained Anger.—In Figs. 22 and 23 we have two terrible examples of the awful effect of anger. The lurid flash from dark clouds (Fig. 22) was taken from the aura of a rough and partially intoxicated man in the East End of London, as he struck down a woman; the flash darted out at her the moment before he raised his hand to strike, and caused a shuddering feeling of horror, as though it might slay.

FIG. 21. SELFISH AMBITION

The keen-pointed stiletto-like dart (Fig. 23) was a thought of steady anger, intense and desiring vengeance, of the quality of murder, sustained through years, and directed against a person who had inflicted a deep injury on the one who sent it forth; had the latter been possessed of a strong and trained will, such a thought-form would slay, and the one nourishing it is running a very serious danger of becoming a murderer in act as well as in thought in a future incarnation. It will be noted that both of them take the flash-like form, though the upper is irregular in its shape, while the lower represents a steadiness of intention which is far more dangerous. The basis of utter selfishness out of which the upper one springs is very characteristic and instructive.

The difference in color between the two is notable. . In the upper one the dirty brown of selfishness is so strongly evident that it stains even the outrush of anger; while in the second case, though no doubt selfishness was at the root of that also, the original thought has been forgotten in the sustained and concentrated wrath. One who studies Plate XIII. in Man Visible and Invisible will be able to image to himself the condition of the astral body from which these forms are protruding; and surely the mere sight of these pictures, even without examination, should prove a powerful object-lesson in the evil of yielding to the passion of anger.

FIG. 23. SUSTAINED ANGER/ FIG. 22. MURDEROUS RAGE

Explosive Anger.—In Fig. 24 we see an exhibition of anger of a totally different character. Here is no sustained hatred, but simply a vigorous explosion of irritation. It is at once evident that while the creators of the forms shown in Figs. 22 and 23 were each directing their ire against an individual, the person who is responsible for the explosion in Fig. 24 is for the moment at war with the whole world round him.

It may well express the sentiment of some choleric old gentleman, who feels himself insulted or impertinently treated, for the dash of orange intermingled with the scarlet implies that his pride has been seriously hurt. It is instructive to compare the radiations of this plate with those of Fig. 11.

Here we see indicated a veritable explosion, instantaneous in its passing and irregular in its effects; and the vacant center shows us that the feeling that caused it is already a thing of the past, and that no further force is being generated.

FIGURE 24 EXPLOSIVE ANGER

In Fig. 11, on the other hand, the center is the strongest part of the thought-form, showing that this is not the result of a momentary flash of feeling, but that there is a steady continuous upwelling of the energy, while the rays show by their quality and length and the evenness of their distribution the steadily sustained effort which produces them.

Watchful and Angry Jealousy.—In Fig. 25 we see an interesting though unpleasant thought-form. Its peculiar brownish-green color at once indicates to the practiced clairvoyant that it is an expression of jealousy, and its curious shape shows the eagerness with which the man is watching its object.

The remarkable resemblance to the snake with raised head aptly symbolizes the extraordinarily fatuous attitude of the jealous person, keenly alert to discover signs of that which he least of all wishes to see.

FIG. 25. WATCHFUL JEALOUSY

The moment that he does see it, or imagines that he sees it, the form will change into the far commoner one shown in Fig. 26, where the jealousy is already mingled with anger. It may be noted that here the jealousy is merely a vague cloud, though interspersed with very definite flashes of anger ready to strike at those by whom it fancies itself to be injured; whereas in Fig. 25, where there is no anger as yet, the jealousy itself has a perfectly definite and very expressive outline.

FIG. 26. ANGRY JEALOUSY

SYMPATHY

Vague Sympathy.—In Fig. 18A we have another of the vague clouds, but this time its green color shows us that it is a manifestation of the feeling of sympathy.

We may infer from the indistinct character of its outline that it is not a definite and active sympathy, such as would instantly translate itself from thought into deed; it marks rather such a general feeling of commiseration as might come over a man who read an account of a sad accident, or stood at the door of a hospital ward looking in upon the patients.

FIG. 18A. VAGUE SYMPATHY

FEAR

Sudden Fright.—One of the most pitiful objects in nature is a man or an animal in a condition of abject fear; and an examination of Plate XIV. in Man Visible and Invisible shows that under such circumstances the astral body presents no better appearance than the physical. When a man's astral body is thus in a state of frenzied palpitation, its natural tendency is to throw off amorphous explosive fragments, like masses of rock hurled out in blasting, as will be seen in Fig. 30; but when a person is not terrified but seriously startled, an effect such as that shown in Fig. 27 is often produced.

In one of the photographs taken by Dr Baraduc of Paris, it was noticed that an eruption of broken circles resulted from sudden annoyance, and this outrush of crescent-shaped forms seems to be of somewhat the same nature, though in this case there are the accompanying lines of matter which even increase the explosive appearance. It is noteworthy that all the crescents to the right hand, which must obviously have been those expelled earliest, show nothing but the livid grey of fear; but a moment later the man is already partially recovering from the shock, and beginning to feel angry that he allowed himself to be startled.

This is shown by the fact that the later crescents are lined with scarlet, evidencing the mingling of anger and fear, while the last crescent is pure scarlet, telling us that even already the fright is entirely overcome, and only the annoyance remains.

FIG. 27. SUDDEN FRIGHT

GREED

Selfish Greed.—Fig. 28 gives us an example of selfish greed—a far lower type than Fig. 21. It will be noted that here there is nothing even so lofty as ambition, and it is also evident from the tinge of muddy green that the person from whom this unpleasant thought is projecting is quite ready to employ deceit in order to obtain her desire.

While the ambition of Fig. 21 was general in its nature, the craving expressed in Fig. 28 is for a particular object towards which it is reaching out; for it will be understood that this thought-form, like that in Fig. 13, remains attached to the astral body, which must be supposed to be on the left of the picture.

Claw-like forms of this nature are very frequently to be seen converging upon a woman who wears a new dress or bonnet, or some specially attractive article of jewellery.

The thought-form may vary in colour according to the precise amount of envy or jealousy which is mingled with the lust for possession, but an approximation to the shape indicated in our illustration will be found in all cases. Not infrequently people gathered in front of a shop-window may be seen thus protruding astral cravings through the glass.

FIG. 28. SELFISH GREED

Greed for Drink.—In Fig. 29 we have another variant of the same passion, perhaps at an even more degraded and animal level. This specimen was taken from the astral body of a man just as he entered at the door of a drinking-shop; the expectation of and the keen desire for the liquor which he was about to absorb showed itself in the projection in front of him of this very unpleasant appearance.

FIG. 29. GREED FOR DRINK

Once more the hooked protrusions show the craving, while the colour and the coarse mottled texture show the low and sensual nature of the appetite. Sexual desires frequently show themselves in an exactly similar manner. Men who give birth to forms such as this are as yet but little removed from the animal; as they rise in the scale of evolution the place of this form will gradually be taken by something resembling that shown in Fig. 13, and very slowly, as development advances, that in turn will pass through the stages indicated in Figs. 9 and 8, until at last all selfishness is cast out, and the desire to have has been transmuted into the desire to give, and we arrive at the splendid results shown in Figs. 11 and 10.

VARIOUS EMOTIONS

At a Shipwreck.—Very serious is the panic which has occasioned the very interesting group of thought-forms which are depicted in Fig. 30. They were seen simultaneously, arranged exactly as represented, though in the midst of indescribable confusion, so their relative positions have been retained, though in explaining them it will be convenient to take them in reverse order.

They were called forth by a terrible accident, and they are instructive as showing how differently people are affected by sudden and serious danger. One form shows nothing but an eruption of the livid grey of fear, rising out of a basis of utter selfishness: and unfortunately there were many such as this. The shattered appearance of the thought-form shows the violence and completeness of the explosion, which in turn indicates that the soul of that person was possessed with frantic terror, and that the overpowering sense of personal danger excluded for the time every higher feeling.

FIG. 30. AT A SHIPWRECK

The second form represents at least an attempt at self-control, and shows the attitude adopted by a person having a certain amount of religious feeling. The thinker is seeking solace in prayer, and endeavoring in this way to overcome her fear. This is indicated by the point of greyish-blue which lifts itself hesitatingly upwards; the color shows, however, that the effort is but partially successful, and we see also from the lower part of the thought-form, with its irregular outline and its falling fragments, that there is in reality almost as much fright here as in the other case.

But at least this woman has had presence of mind enough to remember that she ought to pray, and is trying to imagine that she is not afraid as she does it, whereas in the other case there was absolutely no thought beyond selfish terror. The one retains still some semblance of humanity, and some possibility of regaining self-control; the other has for the time cast aside all remnants of decency, and is an abject slave to overwhelming emotion.

A very striking contrast to the humiliating weakness shown in these two forms is the splendid strength and decision of the third. Here we have no amorphous mass with quivering lines and explosive fragments, but a powerful, clear-cut and definite thought, obviously full of force and resolution. For this is the thought of the officer in charge—the man responsible for the lives and the safety of the passengers, and he rises to the emergency in a most satisfactory manner. It does not even occur to him to feel the least shadow of fear; he has no time for that.

Though the scarlet of the sharp point of his weapon-like thought-form shows anger that the accident should have happened, the bold curve of orange immediately above it betokens perfect self-confidence and certainty of his power to deal with the difficulty. The brilliant yellow implies that his intellect is already at work upon the problem, while the green which runs side by side with it denotes the sympathy which he feels for those whom he intends to save. A very striking and instructive group of thought-forms.

On the First Night.—Fig. 31 is also an interesting specimen—perhaps unique—for it represents the thought-form of an actor while waiting to go upon the stage for a "first-night" performance. The broad band of orange in the centre is very clearly defined, and is the expression of a well-founded self-confidence—the realisation of many previous successes, and the reasonable expectation that on this occasion another will be added to the list.

Yet in spite of this there is a good deal of unavoidable uncertainty as to how this new play may strike the fickle public, and on the whole the doubt and fear overbalance the certainty and pride, for there is more of the pale grey than of the orange, and the whole thought-form vibrates like a flag flapping in a gale of wind. It will be noted that while the outline of the orange is exceedingly clear and definite, that of the grey is much vaguer.

FIG. 31. ON THE FIRST NIGHT

The Gamblers.—The forms shown in Fig. 32 were observed simultaneously at the great gambling-house at

Monte Carlo. Both represent some of the worst of human passions, and there is little to choose between them; although they represent the feelings of the successful and the unsuccessful gambler respectively.

The lower form has a strong resemblance to a lurid and gleaming eye, though this must be simply a coincidence, for when we analyze it we find that its constituent parts and colors can be accounted for without difficulty.

The background of the whole thought is an irregular cloud of deep depression, heavily marked by the dull brown-grey of selfishness and the livid hue of fear. In the center we find a clearly-marked scarlet ring showing deep anger and resentment at the hostility of fate, and within that is a sharply outlined circle of black expressing the hatred of the ruined man for those who have won his money.

The man who can send forth such a thought-form as this is surely in imminent danger, for he has evidently descended into the depths of despair; being a gambler he can have no principle to sustain him, so that he would be by no means unlikely to resort to the imaginary refuge of suicide, only to find on awakening into astral life that he had changed his condition for the worse instead of for the better, as the suicide always does, since his cowardly action cuts him off from the happiness and peace which usually follow death.

The upper form represents a state of mind which is perhaps even more harmful in its effects, for this is the gloating of the successful gambler over his ill-gotten gain. Here the outline is perfectly definite, and the man's resolution to persist in his evil course is unmistakable. The broad band of orange shows clearly that although when the man loses he may curse the inconstancy of fate, when he wins he attributes his success to his own transcendent genius. Probably he has invented a system to which he pins his faith, and of which he is inordinately proud. But it will be noticed that on each side of the orange comes a hard line of selfishness, and we see how this i melts into avarice and becomes mere animal greed, which is also so clearly expressed by the claw-like extremities of the thought-form.

FIG. 32. THE GAMBLERS

FIG. 33. AT A STREET ACCIDENT

At a Street Accident.—Fig. 33 is instructive as showing the various forms which the same feelings may take in different individuals. These two evidences of emotion were seen simultaneously among the spectators of a street accident—a case in which someone was knocked down and slightly injured by a passing vehicle.

The persons who generated these two thought-forms were both animated by affectionate interest in the victim and deep compassion for his suffering, and so their thought-forms exhibited exactly the same colors, although the outlines are absolutely unlike.

The one over whom floats that vague sphere of cloud is thinking "Poor fellow, how sad!" while he who gives birth to that sharply-defined disc is already rushing forward to see in what way he can be of assistance. The one is a dreamer, though of acute sensibilities; the other is a man of action.

At a Funeral.—In Fig. 34 we have an exceedingly striking example of the advantage of knowledge, of the fundamental change produced in the man's attitude of mind by a clear understanding of the great laws of nature under which we live. Utterly different as they are in every respect of color and form and meaning, these two thought-forms were seen simultaneously, and they represent two points of view with regard to the same occurrence.

They were observed at a funeral, and they exhibit the feelings evoked in the minds of two of the "mourners" by the contemplation of death. The thinkers stood in the same relation to the dead man, but while one of them was still steeped in the dense ignorance with regard to super-physical life which is so painfully common in the present day, the other had the inestimable advantage of the light of Theosophy.

In the thought of the former we see expressed nothing but profound depression, fear and selfishness. The fact that death has approached so near has evidently evoked in the mind of the mourner the thought that it may one day come to him also, and the anticipation of this is very terrible to him; but since he does not know what it is that he fears, the clouds in which his feeling is manifested are appropriately vague. His only definite sensations are despair and the sense of his personal loss, and these declare themselves in regular bands of brown-grey and leaden grey, while the very curious downward protrusion, which actually descends into the grave and enfolds the coffin, is an expression of strong selfish desire to draw the dead man back into physical life.

FIG. 34. AT A FUNERAL

It is refreshing to turn from this gloomy picture to the wonderfully different effect produced by the very same circumstances upon the mind of the man who comprehends the facts of the case.

It will be observed that the two have no single emotion in common; in the former case all was despondency and horror, while in this case we find none but the highest and most beautiful sentiments.

At the base of the thought-form we find a full expression of deep sympathy, the lighter green indicating appreciation of the suffering of the mourners and condolence with them, while the band of deeper green shows the attitude of the thinker towards the dead man himself. The deep rose-colour exhibits affection towards both the dead and the living, while the upper part of the cone and the stars which rise from it testify to the feeling aroused within the thinker by the consideration of the subject of death, the blue expressing its devotional aspect, while the violet shows the thought of, and the power to respond to, a noble ideal, and the golden stars denote the spiritual aspirations which its contemplation calls forth.

The band of clear yellow which is seen in the centre of this thought-form is very significant, as indicating that the man's whole attitude is based upon and prompted by his intellectual comprehension of the situation, and this is also shown by the regularity of the arrangement of the colours and the definiteness of the lines of demarcation between them.

The comparison between the two illustrations shown in this plate is surely a very impressive testimony to the value of the knowledge given by the theosophical teaching. Undoubtedly this knowledge of the truth takes away all fear of death, and makes life easier to live because we understand its object and its end, and we realise that death is a perfectly natural incident in its course, a necessary step in our evolution. This ought to be universally known among Christian nations, but it is not, and therefore on this point, as on so many others, Theosophy has a gospel for the Western world.

It has to announce that there is no gloomy impenetrable abyss beyond the grave, but instead of that a world of life and light which may be known to us as clearly and fully and accurately as this physical world in which we live now. We have created the gloom and the horror for ourselves, like children who frighten themselves with ghastly stories, and we have only to study the facts of the case, and all these artificial clouds will roll away at once. We have an evil heredity behind us in this matter, for we have inherited all kinds of funereal horrors from our forefathers, and so we are used to them, and we do not see the absurdity and the monstrosity of them. The ancients were in this respect wiser than we, for they did not associate all this phantasmagoria of gloom with the death of the body—partly perhaps because they had a much more rational method of disposing of the body— a method which was not only infinitely better for the dead man and more healthy for the living, but was also free from the gruesome suggestions connected with slow decay.

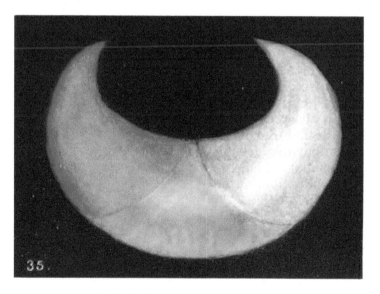

FIG. 35. ON MEETING A FRIEND

They knew much more about death in those days, and because they knew more they mourned less.

On Meeting a Friend.—Fig. 35 gives us an example of a good, clearly-defined and expressive thought-form, with each colour well marked off from the others. It represents the feeling of a man upon meeting a friend from whom he has been long separated. The convex surface of the crescent is nearest to the thinker, and its two arms stretch out towards the approaching friend as if to embrace him. The rose colour naturally betokens the affection felt, the light green shows the depth of the sympathy which exists, and the clear yellow is a sign of the intellectual pleasure with which the creator of the thought anticipates the revival of delightful reminiscences of days long gone by.

The Appreciation of a Picture.—In Fig. 36 we have a somewhat complex thought-form representing the delighted appreciation of a beautiful picture upon a religious subject. The strong pure yellow marks the beholder's enthusiastic recognition of the technical skill of the artist, while all the other colors are expressions of the various emotions evoked within him by the examination of so glorious a work of art.

Green shows his sympathy with the central figure in the picture, deep devotion appears not only in the broad band of blue, but also in the outline of the entire figure, while the violet tells us that the picture has raised the man's thought to the contemplation of a lofty ideal, and has made him, at least for the time, capable of responding to it.

We have here the first specimen of an interesting class of thought-forms of which we shall find abundant examples later—that in which light of one color shines out through a network of lines of some quite different hue. It will be noted that in this case from the mass of violet there rise many wavy lines which flow like rivulets over a golden plain; and this makes it clear that the loftiest aspiration is by no means vague, but is thoroughly supported by an intellectual grasp of the situation and a clear comprehension of the method by which it can be put into effect.

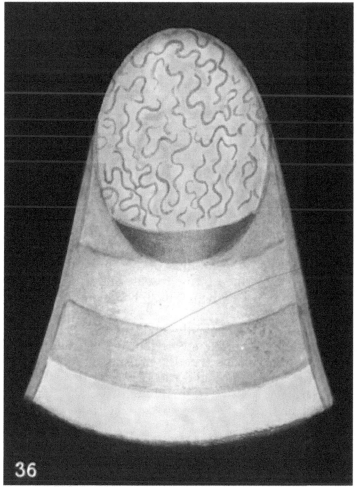

FIG. 36. THE APPRECIATION OF A PICTURE

FORMS SEEN IN THOSE MEDITATING

Sympathy and Love for all.—Hitherto we have been dealing chiefly with forms which are the expression of emotion, or of such thought as is aroused within the mind by external circumstances. We have now to consider some of those caused by thoughts which arise from within—forms generated during meditation—each being the effect produced by a conscious effort on the part of the thinker to form a certain conception, or to put himself into a certain attitude. Naturally such thoughts are definite, for the man who trains himself in this way learns how to think with clearness and precision, and the development of his power in this direction shows itself in the beauty and regularity of the shapes produced.

In this case we have the result of an endeavor on the part of the thinker to put himself into an attitude of sympathy and love towards all mankind, and thus we have a series of graceful lines of the luminous green of sympathy with the strong roseate glow of affection shining out between them (Fig. 37).

The lines are still sufficiently broad and wide apart to be easily drawn; but in some of the higher examples of thought-forms of this type the lines are so fine and so close that no human hand can represent them as they really are. The outline of this thought-form is that of a leaf, yet its shape and the curve of its lines are more suggestive of a certain kind of shell, so that this is another example of the approximation to forms seen in physical nature which we noted in commenting upon Fig. 16.

FIG. 37. SYMPATHY AND LOVE FOR ALL

An Aspiration to Enfold all.—In Fig. 38 we have a far more developed example of the same type. This form was generated by one who was trying, while sitting in meditation, to fill his mind with an aspiration to enfold all mankind in order to draw them upward towards the high ideal which shone so clearly before his eyes.

Therefore it is that the form which he produces seems to rush out from him, to curve round upon itself, and to return to its base; therefore it is that the marvellously fine lines are drawn in lovely luminous violet, and that from within the form there shines out a glorious golden light which it is unfortunately quite impossible to reproduce.

For the truth is that all these apparently intricate lines are in reality only one line circling round the form again and again with unwearied patience and wonderful accuracy. It is scarcely possible that any human hand could make such a drawing as this on this scale, and in any case the effect of its colours could not be shown, for it will be seen by experiment that if an attempt be made to draw fine violet lines close together upon a yellow background a grey effect at once appears, and all likeness to the original is destroyed.

But what cannot be done by hand may sometimes be achieved by the superior accuracy and delicacy of a machine, and it is in this way that the drawing was made from which our illustration is reproduced,—with some attempt to represent the color effect as well as the wonderful delicacy of the lines and curves.

In the Six Directions.—The form represented in Fig. 39 is the result of another endeavour to extend love and sympathy in all directions—an effort almost precisely similar to that which gave birth to Fig. 37, though the effect seems so different. The reasons for this variety and for the curious shape taken in this case constitute a very interesting illustration of the way in which thought-forms grow. It will be seen that in this instance the thinker displays considerable devotional feeling, and has also made an intellectual effort to grasp the conditions necessary for the realisation of his wishes, and the blue and yellow colours remain as evidence of this.

Originally this thought-form was circular, and the dominant idea evidently was that the green of sympathy should be upon the outside, facing in all directions, as it were, and that love should lie at the centre and heart of the thought and direct its outgoing energies.

But the maker of this thought-form had been reading Hindu books, and his modes of thought had been greatly influenced by them.

Students of Oriental literature will be aware that the Hindu speaks, not of four directions (north, east, south, and west), as we do, but always of six, since he very sensibly includes the zenith and the nadir.

Our friend was imbued from his reading with the idea that he should pour forth his love and sympathy "in the six directions"; but since he did not accurately understand what the six directions are, he directed his stream of affection towards six equidistant points in his circle.

The outrushing streams altered the shape of the outlying lines which he had already built up, and so instead of having a circle as a section of his thought-form, we have this curious hexagon with its inward-curving sides.

We see thus how faithfully every thought-form records the exact process of its upbuilding, registering ineffaceably even the errors of its construction.

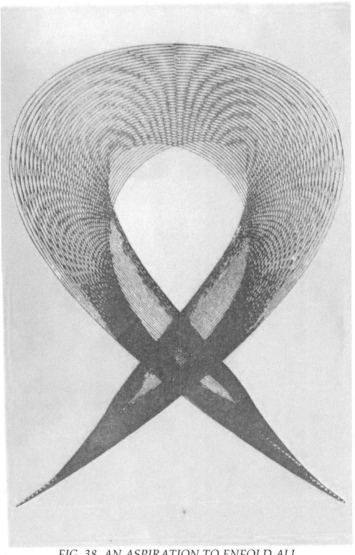

FIG. 38. AN ASPIRATION TO ENFOLD ALL

reading with the idea that he should pour forth his love and sympathy "in the six directions"; but since he did not accurately understand what the six directions are, he directed his stream of affection towards six equidistant points in his circle. The outrushing streams altered the shape of the outlying lines which he had already built up, and so instead of having a circle as a section of his thought-form, we have this curious hexagon with its inward-curving sides. We see thus how faithfully every thought-form records the exact process of its upbuilding, registering ineffaceably even the errors of its construction.

An Intellectual Conception of Cosmic Order.—In Fig. 40 we have the effect of an attempt to attain an intellectual conception of cosmic order. The thinker was obviously a Theosophist, and it will be seen that when he endeavours to think of the action of spirit upon matter he instinctively follows the same line of symbolism as that depicted in the well-known seal of the Society. Here we have an upward-pointing triangle, signifying the threefold aspect of the Spirit, interlaced with the downward-pointing triangle, which indicates matter with its three inherent qualities.

Usually we represent the upward triangle in white or gold, and the downward-pointing one in some darker hue such as blue or black, but it is noteworthy that in this case the thinker is so entirely occupied with the intellectual endeavor, that no color but yellow is exhibited within the form.

There is no room as yet for emotions of devotion, of wonder, or of admiration; the idea which he wishes to realize fills his mind entirely, to the exclusion of all else. Still the definiteness of the outline as it stands out against its background of rays shows that he has achieved a high measure of success.

FIG. 39. IN THE SIX DIRECTIONS

FIG. 40. AN INTELLECTUAL CONCEPTION OF COSMIC
ORDER

The Logos as manifested in Man.—We are now coming to a series of thoughts which are among the very highest the human mind can form, when in meditation upon the divine source of its being. When the man in reverent contemplation tries to raise his thought towards the Logos of our solar system, he naturally makes no attempt to image to himself that august Being; nor does he think of Him as in any way possessing such form as we can comprehend. Nevertheless such thoughts build forms for themselves in the matter of the mental plane; and it will be of interest for us to examine those forms.

FIG. 41. THE LOGOS AS MANIFESTED IN MAN

In our illustration in Fig. 41 we have a thought of the Logos as manifested in man, with the devotional aspiration that He may thus be manifested through the thinker. It is this devotional feeling which gives the pale blue tinge to the five-pointed star, and its shape is significant, since it has been employed for many ages as a symbol of God manifest in man.

The thinker may perhaps have been a Freemason, and his knowledge of the symbolism employed by that body may have had its share in the shaping of the star. It will be seen that the star is surrounded by bright yellow rays shining out amidst a cloud of glory, which denotes not only the reverential understanding of the surpassing glory of the Deity, but also a distinct intellectual effort in addition to the outpouring of devotion.

The Logos pervading all.—Our next three Figures are devoted to the effort to represent a thought of a very high type—an endeavor to think of the Logos as pervading all nature. Here again, as in Fig. 38, it is impossible to give a full reproduction, and we must call upon our readers for an effort of the imagination which shall to some extent supplement the deficiencies of the arts of drawing and printing.

The golden ball depicted in Fig. 42 must be thought of as inside the other ball of delicate lines (blue in color) which is drawn in Fig. 44. Any effort to place the colors in such intimate juxtaposition on the physical plane results simply in producing a green blur, so that the whole character of the thought-form is lost.

It is only by means of the machine before mentioned that it is at all possible to represent the grace and the delicacy of the lines. As before, a single line produces all the wonderful tracery of Fig. 44, and the effect of the four radiating lines making a sort of cross of light is merely due to the fact that the curves are not really concentric, although at first sight they appear to be so.

FIG. 42. THE LOGOS PERVADING ALL

Another Conception.—Fig. 45 exhibits the form produced by another person when trying to hold exactly the same thought. Here also we have an amazing complexity of almost inconceivably delicate blue lines, and here also our imagination must be called upon to insert the golden globe from Fig. 42, so that its glory may shine through at every point. Here also, as in Fig. 44, we have that curious and beautiful pattern, resembling somewhat the damascening on ancient Oriental swords, or that which is seen upon watered silk or moire antique. When this form is drawn by the pendulum, the pattern is not in any way intentionally produced, but simply comes as a consequence of the crossing of the innumerable microscopically fine lines.

It is evident that the thinker who created the form upon Fig. 44 must have held in his mind most prominently the unity of the Logos, while he who generated the form in Fig. 45 has as clearly in mind the subordinate centers through which the divine life pours forth, and many of these subordinate centers have accordingly represented themselves in the thought-form

FIG. 46. THE THREEFOLD MANIFESTATION , FIG. 45. ANOTHER CONCEPTION, FIG. 44. THE LOGOS PERVADING ALL , FIG. 47. THE SEVENFOLD MANIFESTATION

The Threefold Manifestation.—When the form employed in Fig. 46 was made, its creator was endeavoring to think of the Logos in His threefold manifestation. The vacant space in the center of the form was a blinding glow of yellow light, and this clearly typified the First Aspect, while the Second was symbolized by the broad ring of closely-knitted and almost bewildering lines which surround this center, while the Third Aspect is suggested by the narrow outer ring which seems more loosely woven. The whole figure is pervaded by the usual golden light gleaming out between the lines of violet.

The Sevenfold Manifestation.—In all religions there remains some tradition of the great truth that the Logos manifests Himself through seven mighty channels, often regarded as minor Logoi or great planetary Spirits. In the Christian scheme they appear as the seven great archangels, sometimes called the seven spirits before the throne of God. The figure numbered 47 shows the result of the effort to meditate upon this method of divine manifestation. We have the golden glow in the center, and also (though with lesser splendor) pervading the form. The line is blue, and it draws a succession of seven graceful and almost featherlike double wings which surround the central glory and are clearly intended as a part of it. As the thought strengthens and expands, these beautiful wings change their color to violet and become like the petals of a flower, and overlap one another in an intricate but exceedingly effective pattern. This gives us a very interesting glimpse into the formation and growth of these shapes in higher matter.

Intellectual Aspiration.—The form depicted in Fig. 43 bears a certain resemblance to that in Fig. 15; but, beautiful as that was, this is in reality a far higher and grander thought, and implies much more advanced development on the part of the thinker.

Here we have a great clear-cut spear or pencil of a pure pale violet which indicates devotion to the highest ideal, and it is outlined and strengthened by an exceedingly fine manifestation of the noblest intellect.

He who can think thus must already have entered upon the Path of Holiness, for he has learnt how to use the power of thought to very mighty effect. It will be noted that in both the colors there is a strong admixture of the white light which always indicates unusual spiritual power.

FIG. 43. INTELLECTUAL ASPIRATION

Surely the study of these thought-forms should be a most impressive object-lesson, since from it we may see both what to avoid and what to cultivate, and may learn by degrees to appreciate how tremendous is our responsibility for the exercise of this mighty power. Indeed it is terribly true, as we said in the beginning, that thoughts are things, and puissant things; and it behoves us to remember that every one of us is generating them unceasingly night and day. See how great is the happiness this knowledge brings to us, and how gloriously we can utilise it when we know of some one in sorrow or in suffering.

Often circumstances arise which prevent us from giving physical help either by word or deed, however much we may desire to do so; but there is no case in which help by thought may not be given, and no case in which it can fail to produce a definite result. It may often happen that at the moment our friend may be too entirely occupied with his own suffering, or perhaps too much excited, to receive and accept any suggestion from without, but presently a time comes when our thought-form can penetrate and discharge itself, and then assuredly our sympathy will produce its due result. It is indeed true that the responsibility of using such a power is great, yet we should not shrink from our duty on that account.

It is sadly true that there are many men who are unconsciously using their thought-power chiefly for evil, yet this only makes it all the more necessary that those of us who are beginning to understand life a little should use it consciously, and use it for good. We have at our command a never-failing criterion; we can never misuse this mighty power of thought if we employ it always in unison with the great divine scheme of evolution, and for the uplifting of our fellow-man.

HELPFUL THOUGHTS

The Figures numbered 48 to 54 were the results of a systematic attempt to send helpful thought by the friend who has furnished us with the sketches. A definite time was given each day at a fixed hour. The forms were in some cases seen by the transmitter, but in all cases were perceived by the recipient, who immediately sent rough sketches of what was seen by the next post to the transmitter, who has kindly supplied the following notes with regard to them:—

"In the colored drawings appended the blue features appear to have represented the more devotional element of the thought. The yellow forms accompanied the endeavor to communicate intellectual fortitude, or mental strength and courage. The rosy pink appeared when the thought was blended with affectionate sympathy. If the sender (A.) could formulate his thought deliberately at the appointed time, the receiver (B.) would report seeing a large clear form as in Figs. 48, 49, and 54. The latter persisted for some minutes, constantly streaming its luminous yellow 'message' upon B. If, however, A. was of necessity experimenting under difficulty—say walking out of doors—he would occasionally see his 'forms' broken up into smaller globes, or shapes, such as 50, 51, 52, and B. would report their receipt so broken up.

In this way many details could be checked and compared as from opposite ends of the line, and the nature of the influence communicated offered another means of verification.

Upon one occasion A. was disturbed in his endeavor to send a thought of the blue-pink connotation, by a feeling of anxiety that the nature of the pink element should not be misapprehended. The report of B. was that a well-defined globe as in Fig. 54 was first seen, but that this suddenly disappeared, being replaced by a moving procession of little light-green triangles, as in Fig. 53.

These few drawings give but a slight idea of the varied flower-like and geometric forms seen, while neither paint nor crayon-work seems capable of representing the glowing beauty of their living colors."

FIG HT: AURA PHOTOGRAPHY USING AURACAM.

Kirlian photography captures the energy fields around people. This method involves using biofeedback sensors to measure electrical impulses from the skin, which are then translated into colorful images believed to represent a person's aura. Each color is thought to reflect different emotional or spiritual states, like blue for calmness or red for energy.

FIG. 48. HELPFUL THOUGHTS

FIG. 49. HELPFUL THOUGHTS

FIG. 50. HELPFUL THOUGHTS

FIG. 51. HELPFUL THOUGHTS

FIG. 52. HELPFUL THOUGHTS

FIG. 53. HELPFUL THOUGHTS

FIG. 54. HELPFUL THOUGHTS

FORMS BUILT BY MUSIC

Before closing this little treatise it will perhaps be of interest to our readers to give a few examples of another type of forms unknown to those who are confined to the physical senses as their means of obtaining information. Many people are aware that sound is always associated with color—that when, for example, a musical note is sounded, a flash of color corresponding to it may be seen by those whose finer senses are already to some extent developed.

It seems not to be so generally known that sound produces form as well as color, and that every piece of music leaves behind it an impression of this nature, which persists for some considerable time, and is clearly visible and intelligible to those who have eyes to see. Such a shape is perhaps not technically a thought-form—unless indeed we take it, as we well may, as the result of the thought of the composer expressed by means of the skill of the musician through his instrument.

Some such forms are very striking and impressive, and naturally their variety is infinite. Each class of music has its own type of form, and the style of the composer shows as clearly in the form which his music builds as a man's character shows in his handwriting.

Other possibilities of variation are introduced by the kind of instrument upon which the music is performed, and also by the merits of the player. The same piece of music if accurately played will always build the same form, but that form will be enormously larger when it is played upon a church organ or by a military band than when it is performed upon a piano, and not only the size but also the texture of the resultant form will be very different. There will also be a similar difference in texture between the result of a piece of music played upon a violin and the same piece executed upon the flute. Again, the excellence of the performance has its effect, and there is a wonderful difference between the radiant beauty of the form produced by the work of a true artist, perfect alike in expression and execution, and the comparatively dull and undistinguished-looking one which represents the effort of the wooden and mechanical player. Anything like inaccuracy in rendering naturally leaves a corresponding defect in the form, so that the exact character of the performance shows itself just as clearly to the clairvoyant spectator as it does to the auditor.

It is obvious that, if time and capacity permitted, hundreds of volumes might be filled with drawings of the forms built by different pieces of music under different conditions, so that the most that can be done within any reasonable compass is to give a few examples of the leading types.

It has been decided for the purposes of this book to limit these to three, to take types of music presenting readily recognisable contrasts, and for the sake of simplicity in comparison to present them all as they appeared when played upon the same instrument—a very fine church organ. In each of our Plates the church shows as well as the thought-form which towers far into the air above it; and it should be remembered that though the drawings are on very different scales the church is the same in all three cases, and consequently the relative size of the sound-form can easily be calculated. The actual height of the tower of the church is just under a hundred feet, so it will be seen that the sound-form produced by a powerful organ is enormous in size.

Such forms remain as coherent erections for some considerable time—an hour or two at least; and during all that time they are radiating forth their characteristic vibrations in every direction, just as our thought-forms do; and if the music be good, the effect of those vibrations cannot but be uplifting to every man upon

PLATE M. MUSIC OF MENDELSSOHN

whose vehicles they play. Thus the community owes a very real debt of gratitude to the musician who pours forth such helpful influences, for he may affect for good hundreds whom he never saw and will never know upon the physical plane.

Mendelssohn.—The first of such forms, a comparatively small and simple one, is drawn for us in Plate M. It will be seen that we have here a shape roughly representing that of a balloon, having a scalloped outline consisting of a double violet line.

Within that there is an arrangement of variously-colored lines moving almost parallel with this outline; and then another somewhat similar arrangement which seems to cross and interpenetrate the first. Both of these sets of lines evidently start from the organ within the church, and consequently pass upward through its roof in their course, physical matter being clearly no obstacle to their formation. In the hollow center of the form float a number of small crescents arranged apparently in four vertical lines.

Let us endeavor now to give some clue to the meaning of all this, which may well seem so bewildering to the novice, and to explain in some measure how it comes into existence. It must be recollected that this is a melody of simple character played once through, and that consequently we can analyze the form in a way that would be quite impossible with a larger and more complicated specimen. Yet even in this case we cannot give all the details, as will presently be seen. Disregarding for the moment the scalloped border, we have next within it an arrangement of four lines of different colors running in the same direction, the outermost being blue and the others crimson, yellow, and green respectively.

These lines are exceedingly irregular and crooked; in fact, they each consist of a number of short lines at various levels joined together perpendicularly. It seems that each of these short lines represents a note of music, and that the irregularity of their arrangement indicates the succession of these notes; so that each of these crooked lines signifies the movement of one of the parts of the melody, the four moving approximately together denoting the treble, alto, tenor and bass respectively, though they do not necessarily appear in that order in this astral form. Here it is necessary to interpolate a still further explanation.

Even with a simple melody, there are nuances too subtle to fully capture. Each note's line has its own color, so while the outer line appears mostly blue and the next one carmine, both vary throughout. The image shows the general impression rather than every precise tint.

The two sets of four lines which seem to cross one another are caused by two sections of the melody; the scalloped edging surrounding the whole is the result of various flourishes and arpeggios, and the floating crescents in the center represent isolated or staccato chords.

Naturally the arpeggios are not wholly violet, for each loop has a different hue, but on the whole they approach more nearly to that color than to any other. The height of this form above the tower of the church is probably a little over a hundred feet; but since it also extends downwards through the roof of the church its total perpendicular diameter may well be about a hundred and fifty feet. It is produced by one of Mendelssohn's "Lieder ohne Wörte," and is characteristic of the delicate filigree-work which so often appears as the result of his compositions.

The whole form is seen projected against a coruscating background of many colors, which is in reality a cloud surrounding it upon every side, caused by the vibrations which are pouring out from it in all directions.

Gounod.—In Plate G we have an entirely different piece—a ringing chorus by Gounod. Since the church in the illustration is the same, it is easy to calculate that in this case the highest point of the form must rise fully six hundred feet above the tower, though the perpendicular diameter of the form is somewhat less than that, for the organist has evidently finished some minutes ago, and the perfected shape floats high in the air, clearly defined and roughly spherical, though rather an oblate spheroid.

This spheroid is hollow, as are all such forms, for it is slowly increasing in size—gradually radiating outward from its center, but growing proportionately less vivid and more ethereal in appearance as it does so, until at last it loses coherence and fades away much as a wreath of smoke might do. The golden glory surrounding and interpenetrating it indicates as before the radiation of its vibrations, which in this case show the dominant yellow in much greater proportion than did Mendelssohn's gentler music.

The colouring here is far more brilliant and massive than in Plate M, for this music is not so much a thread of murmurous melody as a splendid succession of crashing chords. The artist has sought to give the effect of the chords rather than that of the separate notes, the latter being scarcely possible on a scale so small as this.

It is therefore more difficult here to follow the development of the form, for in this much longer piece the lines have crossed and intermingled, until we have little but the gorgeous general effect which the composer must have intended us to feel—and to see, if we were able to see.

PLATE G. MUSIC OF GOUNOD

Nevertheless it is possible to discern something of the process which builds the form, and the easiest point at which to commence is the lowest on the left hand as one examines the Plate. The large violet protrusion there is evidently the opening chord of a phrase, and if we follow the outer line of the form upward and round the circumference we may obtain some idea of the character of that phrase. A close inspection will reveal two other lines further in which run roughly parallel to this outer one, and show similar successions of color on a smaller scale, and these may well indicate a softer repetition of the same phrase.

Careful analysis of this nature will soon convince us that there is a very real order in this seeming chaos, and we shall come to see that if it were possible to make a reproduction of this glowing glory that should be accurate down to the smallest detail, it would also be possible patiently to disentangle it to the uttermost, and to assign every lovely touch of coruscating color to the very note that called it into existence. It must not be forgotten that very far less detail is given in this illustration than in Plate M; for example, each of these points or projections has within it as integral parts, at least the four lines or bands of varying color which were shown as separate in Plate M, but here they are blended into one shade, and only the general effect of the chord is given.

In M we combined horizontally, and tried to show, the characteristics of a number of successive notes blended into one, but to keep distinct the effect of the four simultaneous parts by using a differently-colored line for each.

In G we attempt exactly the reverse, for we combine vertically, and blend, not the successive notes of one part, but the chords, each probably containing six or eight notes. The true appearance combines these two effects with an inexpressible wealth of detail.

Wagner.—No one who has devoted any study to these musical forms would hesitate in ascribing the marvelous mountain-range depicted in Plate W to the genius of Richard Wagner, for no other composer has yet built sound edifices with such power and decision. In this case we have a vast bell-shaped erection, fully nine hundred feet in height, and but little less in diameter at the bottom, floating in the air above the church out of which it has arisen.

It is hollow, like Gounod's form, but, unlike that, it is open at the bottom. The resemblance to the successively retreating ramparts of a mountain is almost perfect, and it is heightened by the billowy masses of cloud which roll between the crags and give the effect of perspective. No attempt has been made in this drawing to show the effect of single notes or single chords; each range of mimic rocks represents in size, shape, and color only the general effect of one of the sections of the piece of music as seen from a distance.

But it must be understood that in reality both this and the form given in Plate G are as full of minute details as that depicted in Plate M, and that all these magnificent masses of color are built up of many comparatively small bands which would not be separately visible upon the scale on which this is drawn.

The broad result is that each mountain-peak has its own brilliant hue, just as it is seen in the illustration—a splendid splash of vivid color, glowing with the glory of its own living light, spreading its resplendent radiance over all the country round. Yet in each of these masses of color other colors are constantly flickering, as they do over the surface of molten metal, so that the coruscations and scintillations of these wondrous astral edifices are far beyond the power of any physical words to describe.

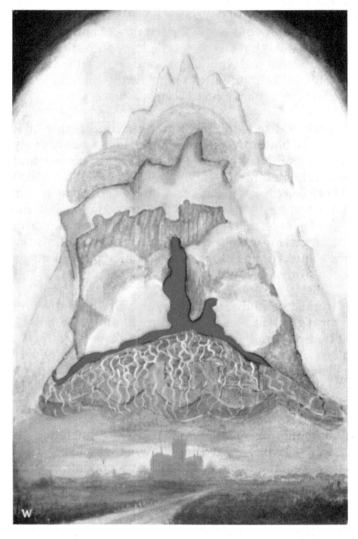

PLATE W. MUSIC OF WAGNER

A striking feature in this form is the radical difference between the two types of music which occur in it, one producing the angular rocky masses, and the other the rounded billowy clouds which lie between them. Other motifs are shown by the broad bands of blue and rose and green which appear at the base of the bell, and the meandering lines of white and yellow which quiver across them are probably produced by a rippling arpeggio accompaniment.

In these three Plates only the form created directly by the sound-vibrations has been drawn, though as seen by the clairvoyant it is usually surrounded by many other minor forms, the result of the personal feelings of the performer or of the emotions aroused among the audience by the music

To recapitulate briefly: in Plate M we have a small and comparatively simple form portrayed in considerable detail, something of the effect of each note being given; in Plate G we have a more elaborate form of very different character delineated with less detail, since no attempt is made to render the separate notes, but only to show how each chord expresses itself in form and color; in Plate W we have a still greater and richer form, in the depiction of which all detail is avoided, in order that the full effect of the piece as a whole may be approximately given.

Naturally every sound makes its impression upon astral and mental matter—not only those ordered successions of sounds which we call music. Some day, perhaps, the forms built by those other less euphonious sounds may be pictured for us, though they are beyond the scope of this treatise; meantime, those who feel an interest in them may read an account of them in the little book on The Hidden Side of Things by Leadbetter.

It is well for us ever to bear in mind that there is a hidden side to life—that each act and word and thought has its consequence in the unseen world which is always so near to us, and that usually these unseen results are of infinitely greater importance than those which are visible to all upon the physical plane.

The wise man, knowing this, orders his life accordingly, and takes account of the whole of the world in which he lives, and not of the outer husk of it only. Thus he saves himself an infinity of trouble, and makes his life not only happier but far more useful to his fellow-men. But to do this implies knowledge—that knowledge which is power; and in our Western world such knowledge is practically obtainable only through the literature of Theosophy.

To exist is not enough; we desire to live intelligently. But to live we must know, and to know we must study; and here is a vast field open before us, if we will only enter upon it and gather thence the fruits of enlightenment.

Let us, then, waste no more time in the dark dungeons of ignorance, but come forth boldly into the glorious sunshine of that divine wisdom which in these modern days men call **Theosophy**.

FIN

NOTES

Please visit other books in the series on Being Human by Neon Zone Press, an imprint of the Decatur Dixon Press.

Made in the USA
Las Vegas, NV
22 November 2024